WINE DOGS

AUSTRALIA

2

more dogs from Australian wineries

Craig McGill and Susan Elliott

A Giant Dog book

WINE DOGS AUSTRALIA 2
MORE DOGS FROM AUSTRALIAN WINERIES

ISBN 978-1-921336-16-4

COPYRIGHT © GIANT DOG, FIRST EDITION 2009
WINE DOGS® IS A REGISTERED TRADEMARK

DESIGNED BY SUSAN ELLIOTT, COPYRIGHT © McGILL DESIGN GROUP PTY LTD, 2009
ALL ILLUSTRATIONS COPYRIGHT © CRAIG McGILL, McGILL DESIGN GROUP PTY LTD, 2009
ALL TEXT NOT ATTRIBUTED, COPYRIGHT © CRAIG McGILL, McGILL DESIGN GROUP PTY LTD, 2009

PROOFREADING AND EDITING BY VICKY FISHER

PRINTED BY 1010 PRINTING INTERNATIONAL LIMITED, CHINA.

PUBLISHED BY GIANT DOG, A.B.N. 27 110 894 178. PO BOX 964, ROZELLE NSW 2039 AUSTRALIA
TELEPHONE: (+612) 9555 4077 FACSIMILE: (+612) 9555 5985
INFO@WINEDOGS.COM WEB: WWW.WINEDOGS.COM

FOR ORDERS: ORDERS@WINEDOGS.COM

OTHER TITLES BY CRAIG McGILL AND SUSAN ELLIOTT INCLUDE:
WINE DOGS: ORIGINAL EDITION – THE DOGS OF AUSTRALIAN WINERIES ISBN 0-9580856-1-7
WINE DOGS: DELUXE EDITION – THE DOGS OF AUSTRALASIAN WINERIES ISBN 0-9580856-2-5
FOOTY DOGS: THE DOGS OF AUSTRALIAN RULES FOOTBALL ISBN 0-9580856-3-3
WINE DOGS AUSTRALIA – MORE DOGS FROM AUSTRALIAN WINERIES ISBN 978-1-921336-02-7
WINE DOGS: USA EDITION – THE DOGS OF NORTH AMERICAN WINERIES ISBN 0-9580856-6-8
WINE DOGS USA 2 – MORE DOGS FROM NORTH AMERICAN WINERIES ISBN 978-1-921336-10-2
WINE DOGS ITALY – THE DOGS OF ITALIAN WINERIES ISBN 978-1-921336-11-9
WINE DOGS NEW ZEALAND – THE DOGS OF NEW ZEALAND WINERIES ISBN 978-1-921336-12-6

HEALTH WARNING: VETERINARY ASSOCIATIONS ADVISE THAT EATING GRAPES, SULTANAS OR RAISINS CAN MAKE
A DOG EXTREMELY ILL AND COULD POSSIBLY RESULT IN FATAL KIDNEY FAILURE. IN THE INTERESTS OF CANINE
HEALTH AND WELLBEING, DO NOT FEED YOUR DOG GRAPES OR ANY GRAPE BY-PRODUCT.

"Every dog has his day..."

——— PROVERB

RED AND **ELLE** 2-YEAR-OLD LABRADORS, ELLENDER ESTATE VIC

CONTENTS

OLLIE THE DOG IS VERY FRIENDLY

FOREWORD

by Nick Ryan

YOU HAVE TO WONDER WHAT THEY'RE THINKING, our fur-coated and flea-collared companions.

What's their view of the winemaking world from the back of the ute?

Does a creature that drinks from the toilet bowl think we're all mad devoting our lives to getting grape juice into a glass?

The bond between winemaker and dog is justly, and for the publishers of this fine and multi-editioned publication profitably, celebrated.

It seems these days that a suitable canine companion is more a pre-requisite for a winemaking career than almost anything else.

Dux of your class at winemaking school?

Big deal.

Worked vintages at Domaine Leflaive, Vega Sicilia and Aldo Conterno?

So what.

Transubstantiated the dripping blood of a Jewish carpenter and turned it into a wine so good a couple of billion people on the planet deny themselves a sleep-in on Sundays?

Couldn't care less.

But turn up for a winemaking job accompanied by an arthritic kelpie with ringworm and a farting problem and you're hired.

You don't see too many axolotls hanging around wineries or guinea pigs lazing about the entrance to cellar door, do you?

And the less said about the bloke from the Barossa who tied up his budgie to the back of the HiLux the better. Poor little bugger managed to keep up all the way from Tanunda down to Lyndoch before his heart blew up in his chest.

So dogs it is.

But why?

I have a few theories and the first one is smell.

A winemaker's livelihood resides deep inside his or her nostrils, the map of their world drawn with aromas and scents.

And dogs dig that. They get it. They respect it.

After all, this is an animal that can pick up a sausage sizzle in the next postcode and chooses sexual partners by sniffing arses, so they know a thing or two and invest a lot in a sense of smell.

And if dogs love their winemakers for a shared sense of smell, I reckon winemakers love their dogs for their total and absolute inability to be judgmental.

These are people whose work is under constant scrutiny. The products of their toil and sweat are constantly put forward for judgment by the wine writers, the show judges and by every single punter who chooses their bottle from a sea of others on the bottle-shop shelf.

But a dog doesn't care if you picked a week too late, has no idea that your ferment got stuck and is completely ambivalent about the fact the bloke down the road got 97 points from Parker and you only got 89.

And best of all dogs don't blog.

Perhaps this unique relationship between winemaker and dog, tighter than young cabernet, is all part of some greater plan.

It's conceivable that the great and good creator, that benevolent being that gave us the glories of pinot noir and the beauty of David Gower's cover drive, the majesty of a sunset over the ocean and the hangover-curing powers of bacon, has engineered this cross-species friendship for a higher purpose.

Maybe he's trying to create the ultimate winemaker.

Just think about it for a minute. As winemakers and their dogs spend more and more time together it's maybe just possible that some of a dog's finer attributes may begin to rub off on their human companions.

How beneficial for a winemaker to have the olfactory precision of a bloodhound, able to drill down into their wines and identify characters not just by vineyard, but by row, vine or even bunch. Hell, they could probably even work out if the pickers had washed their hands.

Imagine a cellar full of winemakers powering through vintage with the energy and enthusiasm of Jack Russell terriers. You wouldn't have excessive staff numbers because only one shift would be needed a day and the savings on coffee alone would put thousands back into the bottom line.

And anyone who has been out drinking with the likes of Andrew Thomas or Joe Holyman and tried to make them go home will understand that they, and too many others like them, could do with a good dash of doggie obedience.

Surely that day will eventually come and when it does, calling a wine a 'dog' may just be the biggest compliment of all.

THROWN OUT OF UNIVERSITY IN ADELAIDE AND MOVING TO SYDNEY, **NICK RYAN** USED THE KNOWLEDGE HE'D GAINED RAIDING HIS OLD MAN'S CELLAR TO LAND A JOB WITH ONE OF SYDNEY'S LEADING WINE MERCHANTS. REALISING THAT WRITING ABOUT IT WAS EASIER THAN LIFTING IT HAS LED HIM TO WHERE HE IS NOW. HE'S A REGULAR CONTRIBUTOR TO *MEN'S STYLE AUSTRALIA, GOURMET TRAVELLER WINE, JAMIE MAGAZINE* AND MANY MORE. HE IS PASSIONATE ABOUT WINES THAT ARE JUST AS INTERESTING BY THE FOURTH GLASS AS THEY ARE AT THE FIRST AND WOULD GIVE IT ALL UP TO PLAY ONE GAME FOR THE PORT ADELAIDE FOOTBALL CLUB.

*"Our dog chases people on a bike.
We've had to take it off him."*

——— WINSTON CHURCHILL

OBSESSION: ROCKS
FAVOURITE TOY: ROCKS
PET HATE: BEING ALONE
FAVOURITE FOODS: COLD LAMB AND BONES
FAVOURITE PASTIME: RELAXING AT THE WINERY
NAUGHTIEST DEED: BURYING BONES IN THE VEGIE GARDEN

SCOOTER

NAUGHTIEST DEED: UNPUBLISHABLE
FAVOURITE PASTIME: RIDING ON THE TRUCK DURING VINTAGE
OBSESSION: FISHING IN THE CELLAR DOOR GOLDFISH POND
FAVOURITE FOOD: ANYTHING THAT HAS BEEN DEAD FOR OVER A WEEK
PET HATES: CATS, POSSUMS AND THREE-TONNE GRAPE BINS ON HIS TAIL

REG

SNOWY

PET HATE: CATS
FAVOURITE FOOD: CHICKEN
OBSESSION: TUMMY RUBS
FAVOURITE PASTIME: SLEEPING
KNOWN ACCOMPLICES: PRINCESS,
TREVOR, RAYMOND, JOYCE AND LYNETTE

PRINCESS

KNOWN ACCOMPLICE: SNOWY
FAVOURITE FOOD: CHICKEN BREAST
FAVOURITE PASTIME: DIGGING HOLES
PET HATES: THUNDER AND LIGHTNING
NAUGHTIEST DEED: EATING CHOCOLATE
OBSESSION: CLIMBING INTO BED TO SLEEP

ROBBIE

OBSESSION: TENNIS BALLS
PET HATE: VACUUM CLEANER
FAVOURITE FOOD: RAW CHICKEN WINGS
KNOWN ACCOMPLICES: JEEPERS AND RUSTY
FAVOURITE PASTIME: SWIMMING IN THE CREEK
NAUGHTIEST DEED: PEEING ON PALLETTED WINE

KNOWN ACCOMPLICE: ZOEY
FAVOURITE PASTIME: DAILY WALKS
FAVOURITE TOY: OLD LEATHER BOOTS
PET HATE: NOT BEING ALLOWED INSIDE
OBSESSION: BEING AS CLOSE AS POSSIBLE
FAVOURITE FOOD: EVERYTHING EXCEPT LETTUCE
NAUGHTIEST DEED: TEARING CLOTHES FROM THE WASHING LINE

ZALA

MONTY

PET HATE: *BEING GROOMED*
FAVOURITE TOYS: *CROQUET BALLS*
KNOWN ACCOMPLICE: *UNCLE WENTWORTH*
OBSESSION: *SWIMMING AT ANY TEMPERATURE*
FAVOURITE PASTIME: *STALKING RABBITS AND DUCKS*
NAUGHTIEST DEED: *SHAKING WATER OVER RESTAURANT DINERS*

WENTWORTH

KNOWN ACCOMPLICE: NEPHEW MONTY
FAVOURITE FOOD: GOURMET SCRAPS
FROM MAYFIELD VINEYARD RESTAURANT
FAVOURITE TOY: R.M. WILLIAMS BOOTS
OBSESSION: BAUME TESTING PINOT NOIR
NAUGHTIEST DEED: RETRIEVING A PEACOCK
PET HATE: BEING TOLD TO RUN INSTEAD OF RIDE IN THE FARM UTILITY

RALPH

PET HATE: BATHS
FAVOURITE FOOD: DUCK
KNOWN ACCOMPLICE: GEORGE THE CAT
OBSESSION: CHASING FEATHERED FRIENDS
UNDER THE VINEYARD NETS DURING VINTAGE
FAVOURITE PASTIME: PLAYING FETCH WITH A BALL
NAUGHTIEST DEED: TRAUMATISING THE NEIGHBOUR'S DUCKS

FAVOURITE PASTIMES: LYING IN THE
SUN AND RIDING IN THE CAR WITH JANE

FAVOURITE FOODS: CHEESE AND RABBIT

OBSESSIONS: RIDING IN THE OLD WINERY
CHEV TRUCK AND CHASING BUTCHER BIRDS

PET HATES: SHOTGUNS, FOXES AND BUTCHER BIRDS

NAUGHTIEST DEED: DESTROYING NUMEROUS FOOTBALL MOUTHGUARDS

DELLA

DUKE

PET HATE: WHEN TIBBI STEALS HIS TOYS
OBSESSIONS: SNIFFING TIBBI'S BOTTOM AND CHASING STICKS
NAUGHTIEST DEED: EATING THE REMOTE AND POWER CORD TO THE NEW TV
FAVOURITE PASTIME: ROCK & ROLL WRESTLING WITH LIVVY, DARCY AND CAM
FAVOURITE TOYS: SOUTH FREMANTLE FOOTBALL AND STUFFED COOKIE MONSTER

OBSESSION: HIS TAIL
FAVOURITE TOY: BUNG
FAVOURITE FOOD: FOOTY FRANKS
NAUGHTIEST DEED: FIVE AM WAKE-UP CALLS
PET HATE: NOT BEING INVOLVED IN EVERYTHING
KNOWN ACCOMPLICES: MAX, ARCHIE, BULLY AND MURPHY

JED

BARNEY

OBSESSION: WOMEN
PET HATE: SWIMMING
FAVOURITE TOY: PEOPLE
KNOWN ACCOMPLICE: WILMA
FAVOURITE PASTIME: CHEWING
NAUGHTIEST DEED: RUINING EVERY PAIR OF SHOES IN THE HOUSE

PET HATE: CATS
OBSESSION: RACHEL
FAVOURITE PASTIME: BARKING
FAVOURITE FOOD: SCHMACKOS
FAVOURITE TOY: SQUEAKING TOY DOG
KNOWN ACCOMPLICES: DRAVEN AND VADAR
NAUGHTIEST DEED: TAKING OFF AND EXPLORING

MAX

RUFUS

PET HATE: AUTHORITY
NAUGHTIEST DEED: BOOT ABDUCTION
OBSESSION: LOUD MOVING MOTORBIKES
FAVOURITE TOYS: VINCE, BALLS AND STICKS
FAVOURITE PASTIME: ATTACKING MOVING MOTORBIKES

OBSESSIONS: RUFUS AND POP
PET HATES: HAIRY MEN AND HOSES
FAVOURITE PASTIME: BEING CUDDLED
FAVOURITE TOY: PLASTIC HAMBURGER
FAVOURITE FOOD: VENISON OSSO BUCCO
NAUGHTIEST DEED: BEING LED ASTRAY BY RUFUS

VINCE

VINCE

OBSESSIONS: RUFUS AND POP
PET HATES: HAIRY MEN AND HOSES
FAVOURITE PASTIME: BEING CUDDLED
FAVOURITE TOY: PLASTIC HAMBURGER
FAVOURITE FOOD: VENISON OSSO BUCCO
NAUGHTIEST DEED: BEING LED ASTRAY BY RUFUS

WILLESPIE WILYABRUP, WA | MONGREL, 1 | OWNERS: THE DURHAM FAMILY

OBSESSION: BUNGS

NAUGHTIEST DEED: LEAVING
BUNGS LYING AROUND

PET HATE: HAVING TO STAY HOME
WHEN THE RESTAURANT IS OPEN

FAVOURITE PASTIMES: PLAYING
WITH BUNGS AND THE ODD ROCK

JACK

RUBY

OBSESSION: *FEET*
PET HATE: *BATHS*
FAVOURITE TOYS: *MANDY'S SHOES*
FAVOURITE FOOD: *KANGAROO MINCE*
NAUGHTIEST DEED: *CHEWING THROUGH HER BEDDING*
FAVOURITE PASTIMES: *SLEEPING AND VINEYARD WALKS*

OBSESSION: GEORGIE'S LEG
FAVOURITE TOY: SOCCER BALL
FAVOURITE FOOD: CHICKEN NECKS
KNOWN ACCOMPLICES: DOT, MISHIE AND BUNJIL THE CAT
FAVOURITE PASTIME: BEING CHIEF OF CELLAR DOOR SECURITY
NAUGHTIEST DEED: BEING OVER-ZEALOUS WHEN WELCOMING VISITORS
PET HATE: SUMMER BURRS IN THE VINEYARD AND THE RESULTANT BATH

JONATHON BIGSLEY

OWNERS: CHRIS AND ANDY MACDONALD | JACK RUSSELL X, 6 | **GUNDAGAI WINES AUSTRALIA** GUNDAGAI, NSW

WOODY

FAVOURITE TOY: PEOPLE
FAVOURITE PASTIME: EATING
PET HATES: BATH TIME AND THUNDER
KNOWN ACCOMPLICES: MUSTI AND CURLY
NAUGHTIEST DEED: WANDERING TO THE MARKET TO BEG FOR SAUSAGES

CURLY FLAT VINEYARD LANCEFIELD, VIC │ TERRIER X, 6 │ OWNER: ROB KOLKKA

OBSESSION: STALKING BIRDS
PET HATE: THE ELECTRIC FENCE COLLAR
THAT KEEPS HIM AWAY FROM BIRD AVIARY
FAVOURITE FOOD: WOOD-FIRED LEG OF LAMB
NAUGHTIEST DEED: WEDGING HIS HEAD BETWEEN
VISITORS' LEGS TO GET HIS BOTTOM SCRATCHED

MUSTI

CURLY

PET HATE: *KIDS WITH STICKS*
FAVOURITE PASTIME: *SLEEPING*
OBSESSION: *GUARDING HER TERRITORY*
NAUGHTIEST DEED: *EATING LUNCH PREPARED BY ANDREW McCONNELL FOR CELEBRATION OF "BEST NEW RESTAURANT"*

FAVOURITE FOOD: RABBIT
FAVOURITE TOY: PEOPLE'S TOES
PET HATE: BEING LEFT AT HOME
OBSESSION: CHASING BLACK SHEEP
KNOWN ACCOMPLICES: MOLLY AND BODHI
FAVOURITE PASTIME: HUNTING FOR MICE, RABBITS AND SILVEREYES
NAUGHTIEST DEED: CHEWING THREE PAIRS OF NEW SHOES IN TWO DAYS

SAVVI

SPOOK

OBSESSION: RON'S UTE
FAVOURITE TOY: FOOD BOWL
FAVOURITE FOOD: WEETBIX
NAUGHTIEST DEED: CHASING THE
NEIGHBOURS WHEN THEY ARE JOGGING
PET HATES: SCARE GUNS AND LITTLE DOGS

OLLIE THE DOG
IS VERY FRIENDLY

OBSESSION: BALLS
PET HATE: BEING LEFT ALONE
FAVOURITE FOOD: CHICKEN NECKS
NAUGHTIEST DEED: DROPPING GAS BOMBS
KNOWN ACCOMPLICES: CHILDREN OF ALL TYPES
FAVOURITE PASTIME: ACTING AS IF HE OWNS THE PLACE

OLLIE

WINSTON

OBSESSION: MUDDY DAMS
PET HATE: OWNER WITH A HANGOVER
FAVOURITE PASTIME: WELCOMING GUESTS
FAVOURITE TOY: ANYTHING THAT SQUEAKS
FAVOURITE FOOD: PORRIDGE WITH LOCAL HONEY
NAUGHTIEST DEED: DESTROYING A THREE-SEATER LOUNGE
KNOWN ACCOMPLICES: MICHAEL, COLLIE, WISTY, MARTIN AND NEIL

FAVOURITE FOOD: SPAG BOL
OBSESSION: BOUNCING BALLS
PET HATE: BEING TAKEN INTO THE SURF
KNOWN ACCOMPLICE: WOODY FROM DRAYTONS
FAVOURITE TOYS: ROPE TUG AND SHERRIN FOOTBALL
FAVOURITE PASTIMES: SUNBAKING AND CHASING BUNGS

DEXTER

HANNAS

OBSESSION: LIZ'S SHOES
FAVOURITE FOOD: LAMB SHANK
FAVOURITE TOY: SQUEAKY BALL
PET HATE: WEARING HIS HALTI COLLAR
KNOWN ACCOMPLICES: BUSTER AND BUNNY
FAVOURITE PASTIME: CHASING DRAGONFLIES
NAUGHTIEST DEED: CHEWING A NEW PAIR OF ITALIAN BOOTS

A MOST DISCERNING DOG

by Dave Powell

THEY SAY THAT NO WINERY is complete without a dog, and things are no different here at our recently completed winemaking facility at Torbreck. Hannas is a 14-month-old German Short-haired Pointer (GSP) who is boisterous, excitable, and inordinately curious about everything (much the same has been said about me!) GSPs are hunting dogs and tend to not only be intelligent, but also right easy to get along with. We have a lot of visitors at the winery, and although young, he fits right in and gets along with everyone.

When not chasing birds, dragonflies, and the occasional kangaroo around the vineyard, he will invariably be found asleep on the big leather sofa in my office. A discussion as to the propriety of the winery dog's presence in the winemaker's office will commence between the two of us; Hannas always wins the argument, resulting in me being the party finding somewhere else to sit. Who's the bigger sweetheart here, anyway?

Hannas can be more than a handful at times. He has a fondness for gnawing on my wife Liz's designer shoes, and he's shown remarkable canine viticultural proclivities by preferring to dine on Shiraz grapes from the vineyards that supply us with fruit for our RunRig flagship wine instead of the more economical Shiraz that we use for the Woodcutter's Shiraz.

These are minor complaints though, when you weigh up his good points, Hannas is a joy to have around, an asset to the vineyard and one of my most favourite companions.

TORBRECK FOUNDER, MANAGING DIRECTOR AND CHIEF WINEMAKER **DAVID POWELL** WAS BORN AND RAISED IN ADELAIDE, SOUTH AUSTRALIA. HE IS A PASSIONATE BELIEVER IN THE BAROSSA VALLEY AND ITS VITICULTURAL HERITAGE.

EDITOR'S NOTE: *FOR ALL ASPIRING WINE DOGS OUT THERE – DO NOT EAT GRAPES AS THEY CAN BE TOXIC OR HARMFUL TO YOUR HEALTH (SEE HEALTH WARNING ON PAGE 2). WINE DOGS FEATURED ARE PROFESSIONAL TASTERS AND DO NOT SWALLOW...*

FAVOURITE TOY: BAZIL
KNOWN ACCOMPLICE: GREAT UNCLE BAZIL
OBSESSION: LYING ON HER BACK AND BEING PATTED
NAUGHTIEST DEEDS: DIGGING HOLES AND EATING SHOES
FAVOURITE PASTIME: LYING ON HER BACK BEING PATTED
PET HATE: NOT BEING PATTED WHEN LYING ON HER BACK

OBSESSION: BARKING FOR FOOD
PET HATE: DINNER BEING LATE (MORE BARKING)
NAUGHTIEST DEED: BEGGING FOR FOOD AT THE CELLAR DOOR
KNOWN ACCOMPLICE: HIS GREAT NIECE POLLY-ANNA PUDDLEDUCK
FAVOURITE PASTIMES: SIGNING WINE DOGS BOOKS FOR A TREAT AND SLEEPING

BAZIL

RUBY:

PET HATE: WATER HOSES
FAVOURITE TOY: HER SOFT TOY MONKEY
KNOWN ACCOMPLICES: ZEPHYR AND LEO
FAVOURITE FOODS: EGGS AND CHICKEN WINGS
OBSESSIONS: CORKSCREWS AND ANYTHING MADE OF METAL
NAUGHTIEST DEED: INAPPROPRIATE USE OF HER COLD, WET NOSE

FAVOURITE PASTIME: CATCHING THE FRISBEE
PET HATES: PLASTIC BAGS AND WATER HOSES
OBSESSIONS: LICKING AND BEING CENTRE OF ATTENTION
FAVOURITE FOODS: BONES AND ANYTHING ANYONE ELSE IS EATING
NAUGHTIEST DEED: DESTROYING COUNTLESS AMOUNTS OF BARREL BUNGS

ZEPHYR

BETTY

FAVOURITE FOOD: YOGHURT MILKSHAKES
OBSESSION: BARKING AT RABBIT HOLES
NAUGHTIEST DEED: HARASSING THE BABYDOLL SHEEP
FAVOURITE PASTIME: GREETING CELLAR DOOR VISITORS
PET HATE: ANYONE WHO WON'T SAY HELLO TO HER AT THE CELLAR DOOR

PET HATE: STAIRS
OBSESSION: FOOD
FAVOURITE TOY: A BIG MARROW BONE
NAUGHTIEST DEED: EATING FRUIT OFF THE VINE
FAVOURITE PASTIME: SWIMMING THROUGH THE SURF
KNOWN ACCOMPLICES: BETTY AND SIDE KICK, THE NEIGHBOUR'S DOG

MOLLY

SMUDGE

FAVOURITE FOOD: BEEF SOUP BONES
PET HATE: PETER LEAVING HER BEHIND
FAVOURITE TOYS: SHOES AND SLIPPERS
OBSESSION: PLAYING TUG OF WAR WITH SLIPPERS
NAUGHTIEST DEED: BEING MUDDY AND THEN ROLLING ON THE BED
FAVOURITE PASTIME: DIGGING HOLES UNDER THE TREES TO SLEEP IN

PET HATE: GOING TO THE VET
FAVOURITE FOOD: AVOCADO SKIN
OBSESSION: GETTING INSIDE THE HOUSE FIRST
NAUGHTIEST DEED: KILLING VANILLA, THE PET RABBIT
FAVOURITE PASTIME: LICKING THE INSIDE OF SALMON TINS

ARROW

FAVOURITE TOYS: THE TWO BLACK CATS

NAUGHTIEST DEED: RUNNING IN A MUDDY
DRAIN NEAR THE HOUSE AFTER A BATH

OBSESSION: PROTECTING THE VINES AND
GRAPES FROM THE BIRDS BY BARKING AT THEM

PET HATE: THE NOISE MADE BY ANGLE GRINDERS

FAVOURITE PASTIME: TRAVELLING IN THE FRONT SEAT OF THE UTE

EVE

OBSESSIONS: MILLIE AND MOGGIE
FAVOURITE PASTIME: BITING MOGGIE'S TAIL
PET HATE: WHEN ANDY PICKS UP THE CAT
KNOWN ACCOMPLICES: MILLIE AND ANDY
FAVOURITE TOYS: MOGGIE AND FOUR-WHEEL MOTORBIKE

TESS

FAVOURITE FOOD: PEDIGREE SMALL DOG FOOD
FAVOURITE PASTIME: CHASING MOGGIE THE CAT
NAUGHTIEST DEED: TURNING ON A WINE TANK TAP
OBSESSION: THE ECHIDNA THAT LIVES BESIDE THEIR YARD
FAVOURITE TOYS: TESS, MOGGIE AND FOUR-WHEEL MOTORBIKE

MILLIE

PINOT

PET HATE: KOOKABURRAS LAUGHING
FAVOURITE PASTIME: WATCHING TV
FAVOURITE FOOD: MARINATED CHEVRE
NAUGHTIEST DEED: CHEWING CUSHIONS
KNOWN ACCOMPLICE: HIS MOTHER, TINA
OBSESSION: STALKING RATS, REAL OR IMAGINED

OBSESSION: CHASING GECKOS
FAVOURITE TOY: HER SON, PINOT
FAVOURITE FOOD: VISITORS' LEFTOVERS
NAUGHTIEST DEED: BARKING AT SHADOWS
PET HATES: SUDDEN NOISE AND MOVEMENT
FAVOURITE PASTIME: SITTING IN FRONT OF THE FIRE

TINA

HARDY

OBSESSION: FRISBEE
NAUGHTIEST DEED: EATING ONE OF EACH
PAIR OF MOTHER-IN-LAW'S FRENCH SHOES
FAVOURITE PASTIME: LYING UPSIDE DOWN ON
THE WARM BRICKS AFTER AN HOUR IN THE PARK
PET HATE: BEING SHOWERED (GOES INTO A TRANCE)

FAVOURITE TOY: TEDDY BEAR
KNOWN ACCOMPLICE: HARDY
OBSESSION: STINGRAY HUNTING
PET HATE: HAVING HIS TAIL BRUSHED
FAVOURITE PASTIME: GETTING PATS FROM EVERYONE.
NAUGHTIEST DEED: EATING A WHOLE BOX OF BELGIAN
VALENTINE'S DAY CHOCOLATES, INCLUDING BOX AND TIN FOIL

SANTIAGO

OBSESSION: *RUNNING WATER*
FAVOURITE TOY: *SQUEAKY FROG*
PET HATES: *VACUUM CLEANER AND COLD MORNINGS*
FAVOURITE PASTIMES: *PLAYING TUG-OF-WAR AND CATCHING RATS*
FAVOURITE FOOD: *BLUE CHEESE WITH QUINCE PASTE ON A BISCUIT*
NAUGHTIEST DEED: *HUMPING A SQUEAKY DUCK TOY AT A DINNER PARTY*

OBSESSION: RABBITS
FAVOURITE TOY: SIZE 2 BUNG
FAVOURITE FOOD: MARROW BONES
FAVOURITE PASTIME: RABBIT HUNTING
NAUGHTIEST DEED: EATING A FOOTBALL
PET HATES: EARLY STARTS AND RABBITS

MURRAY

MERLOT

FAVOURITE TOY: KID'S GUMBOOTS
OBSESSION: GETTING INTO THE HOUSE
NAUGHTIEST DEED: GOING WALKABOUT
PET HATES: THUNDER AND THE RIDE-ON MOWER
FAVOURITE PASTIME: HARRASSING THE HORSE OR BEN
FAVOURITE FOODS: CHEESE, PIG'S EARS AND BEN'S LATTE
KNOWN ACCOMPLICES: THE SHEEP, DESTINY THE HORSE AND CATERPILLAR THE CAT

RED

OBSESSION: ESCAPOLOGY
KNOWN ACCOMPLICE: LARA
NAUGHTIEST DEED: HELPING HIMSELF
TO THE SMOKED PIG'S EAR IN THE PET SHOP
PET HATE: NOT GOING IN THE UTE WITH GRAHAM
FAVOURITE PASTIME: BEING PETTED BY WINERY VISITORS

NELLE

FAVOURITE FOOD: APPLES
FAVOURITE TOY: POLYPIPE OFF-CUTS
OBSESSION: ESCAPOLOGY WITH RED
NAUGHTIEST DEED: CHEWING THROUGH
THE VACUUM CLEANER POWER CABLE
FAVOURITE PASTIME: COMPETING WITH RED FOR
WINERY VISITORS' ATTENTION BY FALLING OVER

WE'RE STILL CHOOSING OUR DOG

by Warren Hately

IT'S BEEN A LONG AND DRAWN-OUT PROCESS. I have to put my hand up as the one at fault. We've had two cats and four children along the way, sort of as a "let's see what this is like before we take any big steps".

You might think that's a foolish approach, but if you've ever been raised with German Shepherds – raised with them, not by them, I might stress – you'd be picky too. Sibling rivalry is bad enough among humans. Try being the youngest in a family fighting for an equal share with three prize-winning show dogs.

So I have to be careful. Make the right decision. A dog is for life. Kids grow up and eventually leave home.

The latest challenge was my wife having twins back about twenty months ago. One of the first lines out of her mouth was "I guess that puts getting a dog back a bit?" A rhetorical question, she was nonetheless right to ask, because it all boils down to me.

It's not the small decision you might think. Then again the newspapers tell me I'm a Libra. One person's indecisiveness is another's careful, methodical approach toward a final, and hopefully perfect, resolution.

The Margaret River area has given us plenty of chances to road test the different breeds. I'm constantly feeding that information into the vast database that will eventually form the impetus for a decision about "the dog". Or an answer to "the dog question," as my father puts it. "Don't rush into it," he warns me. My dad knows I've got terrible patience for anyone smarter than me.

So the kids have been handy so far. A small rowdy pack of children is a good way to tell which mutts are too much for your family and which ones your family would probably freak out and overwhelm.

I've never been one for living vicariously through other people, but other dogs, well that's a whole other question. Rolling up at a local vineyard after work has finished on a Friday armed with just a tennis ball and a stack of sandwiches (for the kids – don't waste haute cuisine on children whose favourite meal is chips and sauce), we've come to rely on those small and not-so-small robust terriers of the winery.

Out they come, trundling down the carefully landscaped entry statement or peeking their heads out from between the actual vines, the scent of children in the air or perhaps it's the incipient sandwiches that make them so inclined.

Based on past experience I am sure most dogs come pre-programmed with the smell of wet tennis ball deep in their genetic memory. A few throws from me and the kids are off, leaving we adults to more genteel pursuits.

Hughie, a local favourite, who isn't technically a wine dog, but I'll soldier on regardless, is one the older kids have come to know and love. He gets about a bit, the old Hughie, and we come across him in town or on the beach at Gracetown or the many other public events that seem so numerous in Margaret River. If ever there was a dog with one whole spectrum dedicated to chasing balls, he'd be it.

Poor guy, you have to force him to take a drinks break or he'd overheat in warm weather doing whatever the kids demand. Eager to please. I like that. He's a classic blue heeler bred with Jack Russell. The effect is to take a perfectly good family dog and then saw half its legs off. His legs in half, I mean. The end result is no less spectacular for all that.

Like many of the mutts in the region, he's got a much bigger spirit than any animal really has a right to possess. A confidence that would make a lesser man blink first.

Perhaps he is the perfect dog.

I'm still thinking about that.

WARREN HATELY IS A MARGARET RIVER-BASED JOURNALIST, WRITER AND PHOTOGRAPHER, AND WAS EVEN A PHILOSOPHY LECTURER IN A FORMER LIFE. HE DOESN'T HAVE A DOG OR HIS OWN VINEYARD YET, BUT ASPIRES TO BOTH, THOUGH HE DOESN'T DRINK AND ISN'T SURE HE HAS THE PATIENCE FOR A PET.

FAVOURITE TOYS: *OTANGA AND RUFFUS*
PET HATE: *NOT GETTING DINNER ON TIME*
OBSESSION: *BEING THE CENTRE OF ATTENTION*
FAVOURITE FOOD: *PORRIDGE AND MILK WITH BICKIES*
NAUGHTIEST DEED: *BITING JESSIE ON THE TAIL AND RUNNING OFF*

JAXON

CHARDY

FAVOURITE TOY: LAMBSY
OBSESSION: SQUEAKY TOYS
NAUGHTIEST DEED: RUNNING AROUND THE
NEIGHBOURHOOD WITH STOLEN UNDERWEAR
FAVOURITE FOOD: BONES FROM THE BUTCHERS
PET HATE: NOT BEING THE CENTRE OF ATTENTION
FAVOURITE PASTIME: BOUNCING ON THE TRAMPOLINE

PET HATE: BEING LEFT OUT
FAVOURITE TOY: ROPE TOY
OBSESSION: CHASING BIRDS
FAVOURITE FOOD: RAW CHICKEN WITHOUT BONES
KNOWN ACCOMPLICES: STORM, MOCHA AND BLUEY
NAUGHTIEST DEED: JUMPING ON TOP OF THE SPA TO LOOK IN THE WINDOW

CHARLIE

KNOWN ACCOMPLICE: JESSIE
OBSESSION: WALKS ON THE BEACH
PET HATES: THUNDER AND PARROTS
NAUGHTIEST DEED: CLAWING THE DOOR
FAVOURITE PASTIME: GOING TO THE BEACH

FAVOURITE PASTIME: EATING
KNOWN ACCOMPLICE: JASPER
PET HATE: NOT HAVING HER TOYS
OBSESSION: PLAYING WITH HER TOYS
NAUGHTIEST DEED: JUMPING UP ON PEOPLE

VOYAGER ESTATE MARGARET RIVER, WA | GOLDEN RETRIEVERS, 14 AND 10 | OWNER: TRACEY THOMPSON-ROURKE

FAVOURITE FOOD: BACON
PET HATE: HAVING HER TAIL PULLED
KNOWN ACCOMPLICES: MAX AND GARY
OBSESSION: CHASING ANYTHING THAT MOVES
NAUGHTIEST DEED: DIGGING HOLES IN THE GARDEN
FAVOURITE PASTIME: WATCHING THE BIRDS FLY BY

CLEO

STELLA

OBSESSION: FOOD
FAVOURITE TOY: ROPE
KNOWN ACCOMPLICE: RAY
PET HATE: VACUUM CLEANER
FAVOURITE FOOD: CHICKEN NECKS
NAUGHTIEST DEED: CHEWING A FRIEND'S SHOE
FAVOURITE PASTIMES: EATING AND WALKING AT THE BEACH

OBSESSION: STICKS
KNOWN ACCOMPLICE: BINDY
PET HATE: BEING LEFT ALONE
FAVOURITE TOY: SQUEAKY PIG
NAUGHTIEST DEED: CHEWING UP SHOES
FAVOURITE PASTIME: FETCHING TENNIS BALLS

OLLY

SAV BLANC
10

FAVOURITE TOY: REPTILES
FAVOURITE PASTIME: RESTING
PET HATE: HER SISTER STEALING ALL THE PATS
NAUGHTIEST DEED: BEING BITTEN BY A REPTILE
OBSESSION: PREVIOUSLY RABBITS... NOW RESTING
FAVOURITE FOODS: FRIED CHICKEN AND SWAMP HEN

MEG

VOYAGER ESTATE MARGARET RIVER, WA | COLLIE X, 11 | OWNER: CHANTELLE CARY

KNOWN ACCOMPLICE: BAM
PET HATE: BEING IGNORED
FAVOURITE PASTIME: SOCCER
FAVOURITE FOOD: LIVE HERRING
FAVOURITE TOY: CHANTEL'S HANDS
OBSESSION: FEMALE DOGS' BOTTOMS
NAUGHTIEST DEED: NIPPING JOGGERS ON THE BOTTOM

OSCAR

ROGER

FAVOURITE TOY: THE CATS
PET HATE: BEING WOKEN UP
OBSESSION: GUARDING HIS BONES
NAUGHTIEST DEED: KILLING CHOOKS
KNOWN ACCOMPLICES: BRUCE AND PADDY
FAVOURITE PASTIME: HANGING OUT OF THE UTE WINDOW

FAVOURITE TOY: ROGER
PET HATE: BEING PREGNANT
FAVOURITE FOOD: SCHMACKOS
FAVOURITE PASTIME: SLEEPING
NAUGHTIEST DEED: RUNNING AWAY
KNOWN ACCOMPLICE: MO THE SHEEP

LISSA

OBSESSIONS: BUNNIES AND CHEESE
FAVOURITE PASTIMES: HANGING AROUND THE
KITCHEN AND LEAVING PUDDLES OF DROOL
PET HATES: MARCH FLIES AND BEING LATE FOR DINNER
FAVOURITE FOODS: SPAGHETTI, CHICKEN AND SCHMACKOS
NAUGHTIEST DEED: STEALING A LOAF OF BREAD FROM THE KITCHEN

MUFASA

FENG SHUI

OBSESSION: CHEESE
FAVOURITE FOOD: PASTA
FAVOURITE TOY: BABE THE PIG
KNOWN ACCOMPLICES: TILLY AND SPARKY
FAVOURITE PASTIME: LONG WALKS WITH TERRI
PET HATE: KIDS ON BIKES AND SKATEBOARDS
NAUGHTIEST DEED: BARKING AT KIDS ON BIKES AND SKATEBOARDS

VOYAGER ESTATE MARGARET RIVER, WA | SHAR PEI X, 8 | OWNER: SANDY THOMAS

BEAR

PET HATE: *OTHER DOGS*
FAVOURITE PASTIME: *SURFING*
FAVOURITE TOY: *FLAT FOOTBALL*
OBSESSION: *CHASING SEAGULLS*
KNOWN ACCOMPLICES: *BONNIE AND CRUZ*
NAUGHTIEST DEED: *STEALING DAVE'S BACON AND EGG BURGER*

FAVOURITE TOYS: MR MEN
OBSESSION: SQUEAKY TOYS
FAVOURITE FODD: HOMEMADE BISCUITS
KNOWN ACCOMPLICE: CHARLIE THE WONDER DOG
NAUGHTIEST DEED: SLEEPING ON HIS BACK ON THE COUCH
FAVOURITE PASTIME: PLAYING WITH STICKS ON THE BEACH
PET HATE: STAYING HOME WHEN EVERYONE GOES TO THE BEACH

SQUID

BONO

OBSESSION: SHADOWS
KNOWN ACCOMPLICE: RAHNI
PET HATE: STAYING AT HOME
FAVOURITE TOY: SQUEAKY TOY
FAVOURITE FOOD: MARROW BONES
NAUGHTIEST DEED: RUNNING AWAY

PET HATE: *BEING WET*
OBSESSION: *RUNNING*
FAVOURITE TOY: *THE CAT*
FAVOURITE FOOD: *CHICKEN*
FAVOURITE PASTIMES: *RUNNING AND SWIMMING*
NAUGHTIEST DEED: *STEALING THE SHOPPING FOR LUNCHES*

BRANDY

ROSA

FAVOURITE TOY: DJANGO
PET HATE: BEING TOLD OFF
KNOWN ACCOMPLICE: CONTO
FAVOURITE FOOD: ROAST LAMB
NAUGHTIEST DEED: CHEWING ON THE HAND-CARVED JARRAH BENCH
OBSESSION: SITTING ON THE GABBEH CARPET THAT SHE'S NOT ALLOWED ON

VOYAGER ESTATE MARGARET RIVER, WA | BORDER COLLIE X, 3 MONTHS | OWNERS: RACHEL KERR AND DEAN TAYLOR

PET HATE: SWIMMING
FAVOURITE FOOD: BBQ CHICKEN
FAVOURITE TOY: GEORGE THE CAT
NAUGHTIEST DEED: DRAGGING THE
CAT AROUND THE HOUSE BY HIS FUR
KNOWN ACCOMPLICES: GEORGE AND JESSIE
FAVOURITE PASTIME: RUNNING ON THE BEACH

CHARLIE

OBSESSION: SOCKS
PET HATE: STAYING HOME
NAUGHTIEST DEED: PULLING NIGEL'S
CHEF'S UNIFORMS OFF THE CLOTHESLINE
KNOWN ACCOMPLICES: ETHAN AND ART
FAVOURITE PASTIME: PLAYING WITH ETHAN AND ART
FAVOURITE TOY: ORANGE BASKETBALL SQUEAKY TOY

PET HATE: RUNNING
FAVOURITE FOOD: CHICKEN
KNOWN ACCOMPLICE: DUTCHY
FAVOURITE PASTIME: SLEEPING
FAVOURITE TOY: ROCKS TO CHASE
NAUGHTIEST DEED: GETTING RUN OVER

KASPA

CHARLIE

PET HATE: NOISE
FAVOURITE TOY: SEAL
OBSESSION: SOFT TOYS
FAVOURITE FOOD: CHEWS
KNOWN ACCOMPLICE: CLEO
FAVOURITE PASTIME: GOING TO THE BEACH
NAUGHTIEST DEED: EATING THE CHRISTMAS TREE AND DECORATIONS

VOYAGER ESTATE MARGARET RIVER, WA | RETRIEVER, 8 | OWNER: HEATHER GROVE

OBSESSION: PLAYING SOCCER
KNOWN ACCOMPLICES: MUM AND BEAR
FAVOURITE PASTIME: CHASING HER TAIL
FAVOURITE TOYS: SOCCER BALL AND HER TAIL
PET HATE: NOT BEING ABLE TO CATCH HER TAIL
NAUGHTIEST DEED: RUNNING AWAY TO JOIN THE CIRCUS

BONNIE

FAVOURITE PASTIME:
NOTHING STRENUOUS
FAVOURITE TOY: PETER'S BOOT
OBSESSIONS: PILLOWS AND BED
PET HATES: THUNDER AND PILL-POPPING
FAVOURITE FOODS: DUCK EGGS AND RODNEY, THE PET BIRD
NAUGHTIEST DEED: EATING DUCK EGGS AND RODNEY, THE PET BIRD

FAVOURITE TOY: GEORGIE'S EAR
FAVOURITE FOOD: PEARS OFF THE TREE
PET HATE: MAGPIES STEALING HER FOOD
FAVOURITE PASTIMES: CHASING RABBITS
AND HANGING OUT WITH THE FIVE BOYS
NAUGHTIEST DEED: ROUNDING UP SHEEP INTO THE DAM
OBSESSIONS: GEORGIE'S EAR AND THE LOUNGE ROOM FIRE

JESSE

OWNERS: JULIE AND PETER MORTIMER | COCKER SPANIEL 6 | **MORTIMERS WINES** ORANGE, NSW

BAILEY

FAVOURITE FOOD: BACON
PET HATE: NAIL CLIPPING
FAVOURITE TOY: YELLOW FOOTY
OBSESSION: YELLOW FOOTY (OR PIECE OF IT)
FAVOURITE PASTIMES: CHEWING AND TUG OF WAR
NAUGHTIEST DEEDS: HARASSING BONNIE AND DIGGING HOLES

OBSESSION: SOCKS
FAVOURITE FOOD: SCOOBY SNACKS
FAVOURITE TOY: SQUEAKY HAMBURGER
FAVOURITE PASTIME: RUNNING NEXT
DOOR TO PLAY WITH SPIDER AND JACKSON
NAUGHTIEST DEED: RUNNING AROUND BALLYCROFT VINEYARD
WITH THEIR ROOSTER IN HIS MOUTH (ROOSTER SURVIVED)

BUSTER

TOBY

KNOWN ACCOMPLICE: SHOLTO
FAVOURITE FOOD: KANGAROO MINCE
PET HATE: OTHER DOGS NEAR HIS BURIED BONES
OBSESSION: CHASING ANYTHING SOMEONE IS WILLING TO THROW OR KICK
NAUGHTIEST DEED: OPENING SLIDING DOORS AND SLEEPING ON THE COUCH

PET HATE: *BEING BRUSHED*
FAVOURITE FOOD: *BBQ CHICKEN*
OBSESSION: *CHASING THE GATOR*
FAVOURITE PASTIME: *RETRIEVING STICKS AND BALLS*
NAUGHTIEST DEED: *TRYING TO EAT MADDIE THE JACK RUSSELL*

BILLIE

MATILDA

OBSESSION: SQUEAKY TOYS
FAVOURITE FOOD: CABANOSSI
PET HATE: THE VACUUM CLEANER
FAVOURITE TOY: NATALIE'S UNDIES
KNOWN ACCOMPLICE: TILLY FROM TINTILLA ESTATE
NAUGHTIEST DEED: RAIDING TATLER WINES' GARBAGE BINS
FAVOURITE PASTIME: SWIMMING IN THE DAM WITH THE DUCKS

90 | **BALLABOURNEEN WINE CO.** POKOLBIN, NSW | AUSTRALIAN CATTLE DOG, 8 MONTHS | OWNER: DANIEL BINET

PRINCESA, DUDA AND...
by Matthew Jukes

PRINCESA WAS BORN IN 2002. She lives in the genteel surroundings of Quinta do Caçador, in the rural Alentejo countryside, near Estremoz in Portugal. She was born from a slightly haphazard and lightning quick relationship between her father, a mongrel-cross Podengo (a surly, ill-educated Portuguese, tailless breed), from the family farm, and her elegant, if rather ferocious, mother, an English, smooth-coated Jack Russell. She was called Pulga and was, by all accounts, 'surprised' one day while touring the vineyards on her daily scout for mice. Princesa (named with more than a touch of irony) is a rough-coated, buff-coloured, right little madam, who nips, snaps, snorts, hunts 'bichos' (bugs and lizards of all sizes) and very much enjoys digging up moles in the perfectly manicured lawn.

Portuguese dogs must earn their living, to a degree, and guarding the estate is supposed to be a twenty-four-hour responsibility. Now, one little, if moody, portly, fuzzy dog is not going to keep away all of the 'stealing bloody gypsies' on her own, so Duda helps out and she lends more than an air of terror in attack for any unsuspecting thieves. Duda is a well-bred Rafeira, brindle (with several broad brushstrokes of cream, black and white) and she's now nudging ten years old. Rafeiros are an Alentejana breed, made popular as guard-dogs by King Carlos of Portugal who realised that they were loyal and gentle-natured but also protective and jolly scary. They live outdoors, even in the winter, and being nocturnal, they patrol at night and woof heartily if anything moves. Females make better guard dogs than the males, so Princesa was extremely happy to welcome Duda to her girl power brigade.

Princesa also liked the fact that Duda wasn't allowed in the house, so she could keep Dona Clara and the maid Idalina to herself – principally for 'doggy love hour' and the staggering number of titbits which Idalina 'dropped by mistake'. These days Duda is occasionally invited into the drawing room, because she's getting on a bit, but even these occasional privileges are not really her bag, not least because the wooden floors are so shiny and slippery and no matter how gingerly she steps she always ends up doing four-corner splits and having to be rescued and helped to the door.

This story takes place some years ago, when an ugly, stumpy, dishevelled, black-and-white, one-eyed dog trotted up the Caçador drive. Seemingly oblivious to its surroundings, clearly on the scrounge, trespassing with an insouciance hitherto unknown on the estate, he not surprisingly got the full treatment – a large, trundling maid twirling a tea towel and howling, a double-dog tsunami of mayhemic woofing and even Dona Clara whispering a few well-turned out expletives.

This happened every day for a week and Princesa and Duda did their duty with alacrity, woofing and chasing the common, if persistent, invader away. They would amble back, tongues wagging several minutes later and Dona Clara would congratulate them on their faithfulness and their reliable, sentry-like behaviour. However, when this annoyingly regular visitor started to take up five, ten and then twenty odd minutes each day, Dona Clara decided to investigate. She waited for that particular afternoon's visitation (you could almost set your watch by it) from the grotty, unkempt little rascal and then watched while Princesa and Duda saw him off (a little half-heartedly?) and she followed. Just beyond the kitchen garden she peered out from behind a tree and was amazed at what she saw – the three dogs frolicking on the grass with gay abandon and then ten minutes later saying 'see you tomorrow' and then returning to the Quinta all ready to pretend that they'd given the scoundrel a proper beating.

So shocked and delighted was Dona Clara that she decided to allow this one-eyed little pirate to stay. He had probably lost his eye to his previous owner's lack of shotgun discipline. He was skittish and wary of humans, but he didn't mind living in an upturned barrel and he proved very adept at keeping rabbits off the lettuces. He loves long walks through the surrounding cork forests and vineyards and in spite of his Cyclops impediment he is very fast and he catches more hares than the other two put together.

He was named Amigo and he seemed immediately grateful for his adoption. These days he loves to be scratched and patted by friends and family, for a few minutes each day (not the full hour), proving that he really is, as his name suggests, a true friend.

MATTHEW JUKES IS THE WINNER OF THE INTERNATIONAL WINE AND SPIRIT COMPETITION'S TROPHY FOR COMMUNICATOR OF THE YEAR AND HAS BEEN WINE CORRESPONDENT FOR THE *DAILY MAIL* AND *MONEYWEEK*. HE SPENT THREE YEARS ON THE BBC WITH HIS WEEKLY WINE SHOW AND HAS WRITTEN SEVEN BEST-SELLING WINE GUIDES. CURRENT BOOK TITLES INCLUDE *THE WINE BOOK*, (HEADLINE), AND *TASTE FOOD AND WINE 2009*, (WINNER OF THE AUSTRALIAN FOOD MEDIA 'BEST FOOD AND WINE WRITING' AWARD). WWW.MATTHEWJUKES.COM

BRANDY

FAVOURITE FOOD: BONES
FAVOURITE TOY: TOY DUCK
KNOWN ACCOMPLICE: REMY
FAVOURITE PASTIMES: CHASING BALLS
AND FRISBEES AND SWIMMING
PET HATE: NOT BEING ALLOWED IN THE POOL

FAVOURITE TOY: BALLS
KNOWN ACCOMPLICE: BRANDY
OBSESSIONS: CHICKENS AND RABBITS
FAVOURITE PASTIME: ROUNDING UP THE CHICKENS
PET HATE: NOT BEING ALLOWED TO CHASE THE CATTLE
NAUGHTIEST DEED: BITING HIS SISTER BRANDY PLAYFULLY

REMY

SPARKS

OBSESSION: CHASING RABBITS
PET HATE: THE NEIGHBOUR'S CAT
FAVOURITE TOY: BRENDON'S DIRTY SOCKS
FAVOURITE PASTIMES: BEING A BIG SMOOCHER
AND CRUISING ON THE BACK OF THE UTE
NAUGHTIEST DEED: GETTING INTO A FIGHT
WITH A KANGAROO AND COMING OFF SECOND BEST

OBSESSION: HUNTING
PET HATES: CATS AND BEING COLD
FAVOURITE PASTIME: LYING IN THE SUN
FAVOURITE FOOD: EATING GRAPES DURING HARVEST
NAUGHTIEST DEED: TANGLING WITH KANGAROOS
AND NEEDING AN EXPENSIVE TWO-HOUR OPERATION

MAZI

PET HATE: BEING LEFT OUT
KNOWN ACCOMPLICE: BOBBY
FAVOURITE FOOD: KANGAROO POO
FAVOURITE PASTIME: CHEWING STUFF
FAVOURITE TOYS: DRIED LEAVES AND FROGS
NAUGHTIEST DEED: CHEWING ELECTRICAL CABLES
OBSESSIONS: SHOES WITH LACES AND NEWSPAPERS

CHARLIE

OBSESSION: GUNS
FAVOURITE FOOD: BILTONG
FAVOURITE PASTIME: SHOOTING
FAVOURITE TOY: TOY AIREDALE PUPPY
NAUGHTIEST DEEDS: HOGGING THE COUCH
AND BAD TABLE MANNERS (ENCOURAGED BY RYAN)

PET HATE: CATS
FAVOURITE TOY: SHOES
OBSESSION: RIDING MOTORBIKES
FAVOURITE PASTIME: BEING HEAD OF SECURITY
NAUGHTIEST DEED: EATING DINNER OFF THE DINING ROOM TABLE

FERMOY ESTATE, WILYABRUP, WA | AIREDALE TERRIERS, 9 AND 4 | OWNERS: THE KELLY FAMILY

OBSESSION: GUNS
FAVOURITE FOOD: BILTONG
FAVOURITE PASTIME: SHOOTING
FAVOURITE TOY: TOY AIREDALE PUPPY
NAUGHTIEST DEEDS: HOGGING THE COUCH
AND BAD TABLE MANNERS ENCOURAGED BY RYAN

SUSIE

FLOYD

OBSESSION: SWIMMING
KNOWN ACCOMPLICE: BUKSIE
FAVOURITE PASTIME: CHASING
KANGAROOS AROUND THE VINEYARD
FAVOURITE TOY: ANY BALL OR STICK
PET HATES: THUNDER AND LIGHTNING
NAUGHTIEST DEED: CHEWING SUNGLASSES

BEAR

FAVOURITE TOY: BOYD'S LEG
OBSESSION: DIGGING HOLES
FAVOURITE PASTIME: SLEEPING
NAUGHTIEST DEED: EATING THE NEW LOUNGE SUITE
PET HATES: VACUUM CLEANER AND TURNING WHEELS

FAVOURITE TOY: BEAR
PET HATE: TEA TOWELS
FAVOURITE FOOD: YOURS
OBSESSIONS: GOING FOR A WALK AND DIANA ROSS
NAUGHTIEST DEED: CHEWING THE LEGS OFF THE KITCHEN TABLE

JEDDA

BRONSON

FAVOURITE FOOD: SLOP
FAVOURITE TOY: TENNIS BALLS
FAVOURITE PASTIME: GALUMPHING
PET HATE: NOT BEING FED ON TIME
KNOWN ACCOMPLICES: SASHA, SALLY AND BLOB
OBSESSION: GROWING UP TO BE A MAN-EATING CROCODILE

FAVOURITE TOY: WOOD CHOCK
OBSESSION: COLIN, HIS MASTER
NAUGHTIEST DEED: EATING FERMENTING GRAPES
KNOWN ACCOMPLICES: ANDY, TIM AND WARWICK
PET HATE: HAVING TO SHARE COLIN WITH ANYONE
FAVOURITE FOODS: KANGAROO AND A GOOD BONE
FAVOURITE PASTIME: WELCOMING PEOPLE TO THE CELLAR DOOR

SAM

AYESHA

FAVOURITE FOOD: BONES
FAVOURITE TOY: BALL ON A ROPE
OBSESSIONS: BIRDS AND KANGAROOS
PET HATE: NOT BEING ALLOWED IN THE CAR
FAVOURITE PASTIMES: PLAYING, CHASING, SWIMMING
NAUGHTIEST DEED: STEALING MEAT FROM THE KITCHEN

PET HATE: *BEING WASHED WITH THE GARDEN HOSE*
NAUGHTIEST DEED: *PICKING HIS OWN TOMATOES AND STRAWBERRIES OUT OF THE GARDEN AND EATING THEM*
FAVOURITE FOOD: *CHICKEN NECKS WITH A SIDE DISH OF TOMATO*
FAVOURITE PASTIMES: *GOING FOR A WALK AND GIVING HIGH-FIVES*
OBSESSION: *COMING TO THE WINERY DURING TIRAGE CULTURE CHECKS*

BO

OWNER:

FAVOURITE TOY: MAC
OBSESSION: THE CAR
FAVOURITE FOOD: SCHMACKOS
PET HATE: NOT GOING IN THE CAR
FAVOURITE PASTIME: TRAVELLING IN THE CAR
KNOWN ACCOMPLICES: MAC AND TOMMY THE CALF
NAUGHTIEST DEED: EATING THE BEDROOM CURTAINS

BUD

FAVOURITE TOY: BUD
OBSESSION: RECEIVING PATS AND CUDDLES
FAVOURITE PASTIME: MAKING NEW FRIENDS
PET HATE: BEING SECOND AT THE FOOD BOWL
NAUGHTIEST DEED: EATING SEQUINNED SLIPPERS
KNOWN ACCOMPLICES: BUD AND TOMMY THE CALF

MAC

GEORGE

PET HATE: CATS

NAUGHTIEST DEED:
RAIDING LUNCH BOXES

KNOWN ACCOMPLICES:
VISITORS WITH FOOD

FAVOURITE PASTIME:
ESCORTING THE FORKLIFT

ME AND MY SHADOW
by Peter Lehmann

BRONSON WAS MY SHADOW. He weighed the grapes with me in the Weighbridge, he sat under my desk in the office, went to all winery functions and naturally attended all Board meetings. Dead on the dot of noon, Bronson would rise from under the table, brush the Chairman's knee with intent and ask to be let out. The Chairman, Des Ross, used to say Bronson always knew exactly when Board discussion started to get off the point and it was a perfect signal to close the meeting.

When we went away for a week or so, we always left Bronson in the care of our Cellar Foreman, Lynton Pritchard, whose nick name is "Two Dogs". Lynton would bring him to work as per usual (and was naturally dubbed "Three Dogs"), Bronson would happily wander through the cellars with Lynton and always be by his side. Except on the day we were due home. He'd leave Lynton and go to the bottom warehouse and wait, not moving until he saw our car coming around the corner.

How on earth did he know this was the appointed day? Blowed if we do!

As amazing as we all thought Bronson was, he was even recognised by The Australian Wine Selector – they named him the 2002 winner of "Man's Best Friend". We still have the engraved bowl.

PETER LEHMANN HAS BEEN DESCRIBED AS ONE OF AUSTRALIA'S MOST RESPECTED AND INNOVATIVE WINE MAKERS. FOUNDED IN 1979, PETER LEHMANN WINES PRODUCES AROUND 600,000 CASES ANNUALLY. THE EMINENT WINE WRITER, JAMES HALLIDAY, WROTE OF PETER LEHMANN: "IT IS NOT OFTEN THAT A PERSON BECOMES A LEGEND IN HIS OWN LIFETIME." PETER LEHMANN IS INDEED A LEGEND IN THE AUSTRALIAN WINE INDUSTRY AND HE IS KNOWN, WITH AFFECTION AND RESPECT, AS THE "BARON OF THE BAROSSA".

FAVOURITE TOY: BALLS
KNOWN ACCOMPLICE: HIS BROTHER JACK
FAVOURITE PASTIMES: EATING AND SLEEPING
PET HATE: KANGAROOS WHO ENTER THE VINEYARDS
FAVOURITE FOOD: EVERYTHING - HIS NICKNAME IS HOOVER
NAUGHTIEST DEED: BARKING AT KANGAROOS IN THE EARLY HOURS

ZAC

FAVOURITE TOY: STICKS
FAVOURITE FOOD: CHICKEN
PET HATE: STRONZA THE WINERY CAT
KNOWN ACCOMPLICE: ZAC, HIS OLDER BROTHER
NAUGHTIEST DEED: DIGGING BIG HOLES IN THE GARDEN
FAVOURITE PASTIMES: GREETING GUESTS AND SWIMMING IN THE RIVER
OBSESSION: MAKING SURE THE FOUR-WHEEL DRIVE GOES NOWHERE WITHOUT HIM

JACK

SALLY

PET HATE: BEING LEFT ALONE
NAUGHTIEST DEED: LYING IN THE
WAY SO PEOPLE TRIP OVER HER
FAVOURITE PASTIMES: SLEEPING AND EATING
OBSESSIONS: SLEEPING AND BEING VERY CLOSE TO FAMILY
KNOWN ACCOMPLICES: MOLLY, MONTY AND OSKAR THE CAT

FAVOURITE TOY: CUSTOMERS' FOOTY
FAVOURITE PASTIMES: SLEEPING AND
GETTING PATS FROM CUSTOMERS
NAUGHTIEST DEED: PUNCTURING
A CUSTOMER'S FOOTY
PET HATES: BATH TIME
AND GOING TO THE VET
FAVOURITE FOODS:
CHOPS AND GRAVY

JACK

NERO

PET HATE: DIETING
OBSESSION: FOOD, GLORIOUS FOOD
FAVOURITE FOOD: FRESHLY CAUGHT LIVE RABBITS
FAVOURITE TOY: ANY OLD BONE (PREFERABLY FROM A DEAD COW)
FAVOURITE PASTIME: WAITING FOR LUNCH, BREAKFAST AND DINNER
NAUGHTIEST DEED: DIGGING UP DEAD COWS AT MIDNIGHT WITH BACCHUS
KNOWN ACCOMPLICE: BACCHUS, HIS KENNEL MATE AND PARTNER IN CRIME

PET HATE: HAVING A BATH
FAVOURITE FOOD: MEATBALLS
OBSESSION: HERDING THE GATOR
FAVOURITE PASTIME: HAVING HIS TUMMY RUBBED
NAUGHTIEST DEED: DIGGING UP DEAD COWS AT MIDNIGHT WITH NERO

BACCHUS

FAVOURITE FOOD: THE CAT'S
FAVOURITE TOYS: BALL AND STICKS
PET HATE: BEING WASHED WITH THE HOSE
FAVOURITE PASTIME: PLAYING WITH MADELEINE
OBSESSION: CHASING ANYTHING WITH WHEELS
NAUGHTIEST DEED: CHASING THE POSTIE'S BIKE
KNOWN ACCOMPLICE: LOLA THE THREE-LEGGED CAT

SHEP

OBSESSION: LYING IN THE SUN
FAVOURITE FOOD: HUMAN FOOD
PET HATE: BEING LEFT ALONE INSIDE THE HOUSE
FAVOURITE PASTIME: MEETING AND GREETING AT THE CELLAR DOOR
NAUGHTIEST DEED: CHASING THE PEACOCKS WHEN THEY ARE NEAR HIS BONE

CHILLI

KIRRA

FAVOURITE TOY: HER LANDCRUISER
FAVOURITE PASTIME: FETCHING STICKS
KNOWN ACCOMPLICES: MAYA AND ZOE
NAUGHTIEST DEED: JUMPING ON WINERY VISITORS
PET HATE: THE VISITING KANGAROOS ON HER TURF
OBSESSION: ANY KIND OF FOOD INCLUDING TENNIS BALLS

DARK EYES WARRAGAMBA
AKA NAPOLEON BONAPARTE

by Greg Duncan Powell

THE WHOLE BUDDHIST NOTION about souls being eternally recycled into animals, bugs, beetles etc is one that is perspicacious to ponder but difficult to prove, and God only knows where the soul of Napoleon Bonaparte went after he died on St Helena on 5 May 1821, but I do know for a fact that it turned up some 151 years later in a suburb of Canberra in the body of our Australian silky terrier.

Had I known a little more French history when I was ten I probably would have recognised Monsieur Bonaparte in the little puppy we took home in 1972. In a litter of six pups, 'Dark Eyes Warragamba' (all the pups in the litter were named after NSW dams) was quiet, reserved, dignified and a whole lot less yappy than his siblings, which is just as historians describe Napoleon in his youth.

Warra grew into a good dog, albeit a terrier with a Napoleonic personality. He was extremely fussy about food, preferring French cheeses and expensive small goods to traditional canine fare. He would turn his nose up and look disgusted if you offered him dog food, mince or a juicy beef bone but he might be tempted by a stinky morsel of ripe Roquefort or a slice of pepperoni.

When it came to romance, Warra's Josephine was a bitch down the road. She was a pretty, long-haired dachshund by the name of Gypsy, which was odd because she never went anywhere. It was Warra who was the gypsy and would invariably manage to escape barracks and linger around Gypsy's house weeing on car tyres and the nose of his main rival, a fox terrier named Jasper.

Napoleon had a liking for big hats, large horses, high heels and world domination and Warra had the same small man (or small dog) complex. He would use his abundant silky hair and no small amount of burrs and dags to increase his bulk. It was the canine equivalent of big hair. Rolling in dung and other aromatic nasties would give him dreads, a rasta-like look and fluff him up to double his size. But the kryptonite was water, which would flatten his hairdo and show off his true, rat-like, puny form.

Consequently Warra hated rain, swimming, baths and liquids in general, apart from his own urine, which he would eke out by the drop on everything that stood higher than a blade of grass.

Eventually the aroma of the rasta hairdo would become too much for us and we would give Warra a hair cut. This was no simple groom-the-pooch routine – for Warra it was a tragedy, very much like what happened to Elvis when he went into the army. To get rid of all the dags and matted-up hair Warra got the number one all over. His response was equivalent to Napoleon's during his first exile on Elba: abject humiliation. He would hide away, shaking in frustration and pity in a cupboard underneath the TV until his hair grew back or he could at least roll in something stinky.

But all this was nothing by comparison with Warra/Napoleon's bellicose behaviour. Socially, a friendly dog but when it came to territory Warra considered himself ruler of an empire that had no limits. Always with reserves in his bladder he would mark his ever-expanding world assiduously and defend it to his (or our) death. And just as Napoleon embarked on hopelessly outnumbered campaigns with his impoverished Grande Armée against the might of Austria and Britain, Warra would pick fights against the biggest, meanest dogs.

Unlike Napoleon, Warra never won. He lost every single fight and got terribly beat up in the process. Brutish blue heelers would grab him by the neck and shake him like a rag doll until we managed to pry him from the beast's teeth. We'd take him to the vet, get him stitched up, think that he'd learnt his lesson but just like the Corsican crusader he would simply try a different strategy or a different opponent, a German Shepherd or Rottweiler with the same result.

Surprisingly Warra managed to survive to old age without amending his behaviour. Held together by stitches, and walking a bit gingerly from all the beatings, he'd been exiled to Sandy Bay in Tasmania with my parents and it was there on a cold wintry day that he died, not at the hands of the enemy but a car that got in the way of his initial cavalry charge.

Those who have been to the fantastic military museum in Paris known as Les Invalides will have seen Napoleon's tomb. It's a giant thing, bigger than a cement truck in the middle of the foyer. One looks at it and cannot help but think about all the spare real estate inside. Napoleon's human remains must occupy only one corner. The vestiges of his canine form are in a place that is probably a little less grand but no less scenic. Warra/Napoleon's earthly remains now reside beneath a large crimson camellia overlooking the entrance to the Derwent River. What form his spirit has taken now is anyone's guess. Anyone with a pugnacious budgie?

GREG DUNCAN POWELL HAS BEEN WRITING ABOUT WINE AND OTHER DRINKS FOR MOST OF HIS ADULT LIFE. CURRENTLY HE IS DRINKS EDITOR FOR *VOGUE ENTERTAINING + TRAVEL*, HAS A COLUMN IN *GRAZIA* AND WRITES LOADS OF BOOKS. HIS MOST RECENT WORKS ARE *BEER – A GAUGE FOR ENTHUSIASTS* (MURDOCH BOOKS) AND THE EQUALLY SELF-EXPLANATORY *BREAKFAST* (MURDOCH BOOKS). A DOG LOVER FROM WAY BACK, HE'S CURRENTLY IN THE MARKET FOR A NEW POOCH.

KALI

OBSESSION: UNDERWEAR
KNOWN ACCOMPLICE: LINCOLN
PET HATE: BEING LEFT AT HOME
FAVOURITE PASTIME: SWIMMING
NAUGHTIEST DEED: SNEAKING OFF
FAVOURITE TOYS: ANY STICK OR BALL

FAVOURITE TOY: GLOVE
OBSESSION: UNDERWEAR
KNOWN ACCOMPLICE: KALI
FAVOURITE FOOD: CHOCOLATE
FAVOURITE PASTIME: SWIMMING
PET HATE: NOT BEING SPOKEN TO IN THE MORNING
NAUGHTIEST DEED: RIPPING THE UTE'S VINYL UPHOLSTERY APART

LINCOLN

KNOWN ACCOMPLICES:
BELLA, DARCY AND DEEVER
PET HATE: NOT GETTING ENOUGH FOOD
FAVOURITE PASTIME: HAVING ADVENTURES AT THE TAMAR RIVER

FAVOURITE PASTIME: SWIMMING IN THE TAMAR RIVER WITH PINOT THE PIG

NAUGHTIEST DEED: LEADING THE PIG ASTRAY AND GETTING HIM LOST

BELLA

PINOT

OBSESSION: BECOMING
A CERTIFIED ORGANIC
VITICULTURAL WORKER

NAUGHTIEST DEED:
ROLLING IN MUD THEN
GREETING CELLAR DOOR CUSTOMERS

OBSESSION: TAKING OFF WITH BUNGS
KNOWN ACCOMPLICES: PINOT, DARCY AND DEEVER
PET HATE: THE PIG BEING ALLOWED TO EAT ANYTHING

BELLA

CELLAR DOOR SALES

...ER TREE
...WINES
VINTAGE
UPDATE
...AY...
...HING
SHIRAZ

OBSESSION: *BOB THE RABBIT (RIP)*
FAVOURITE FOOD: *PEOPLE FOOD*
NAUGHTIEST DEED: *RUNNING AWAY AND BECOMING A HOBO*
KNOWN ACCOMPLICE: *MAXI*
PET HATE: *PEOPLE MOVING IN SLOW MOTION*
FAVOURITE TOY: *BOB*

KIMBA

OSCAR

PET HATE: *LIGHTNING*

OBSESSION: *ATTENTION*

KNOWN ACCOMPLICE: *FELIX*

FAVOURITE PASTIMES: *SNIFFING,*
LICKING AND CHEWING EVERYTHING

NAUGHTIEST DEED: *CHEWING THROUGH*
THE BRAKE CABLE ON DANIELA'S CAR

FAVOURITE TOY: BONES
PET HATE: NOT BEING FED ON TIME
OBSESSIONS: FOOD, STICKS AND BALLS
FAVOURITE PASTIMES: EATING AND SLEEPING
NAUGHTIEST DEED: ESCAPING TO THE BEACH ACROSS THE ROAD

FELIX

OWNERS: JEREMY AND DANIELA GORDON | LABRADOR 8 | FLAMETREE WINES DUNSBOROUGH WA | 127

FAVOURITE FOOD: MULBERRIES
FAVOURITE PASTIME: CUDDLING
NAUGHTIEST DEED: CHASING AND
CATCHING THE NEIGHBOURS' SHEEP
PET HATE: SMALL AND NOISY CHILDREN
OBSESSION: CHASING BIRDS OUT OF THE NETS

FAVOURITE FOOD: APRICOTS
OBSESSION: FETCH, FETCH, FETCH
PET HATE: SMALL WHITE FLUFFY DOGS
NAUGHTIEST DEED: SWALLOWING A BONE AND
NEEDING MAJOR THORACIC SURGERY AS A RESULT

FAVOURITE TOY: BARREL BUNG
OBSESSION: CHEWING STICKS AND BRANCHES
KNOWN ACCOMPLICES: BRUCE, JACK AND RORY
PET HATE: NOT BEING ALLOWED TO BEG IN THE RESTAURANT
NAUGHTIEST DEED: CLEANING UP AFTER REUBEN, THE WINERY PEACOCK

MOLLY

DIGGER

FAVOURITE TOY: BALL

FAVOURITE FOOD: PIZZA

OBSESSION: STEALING FOOD FROM
THE VINEYARD BOYS' LUNCH BOXES

NAUGHTIEST DEED: LUNCH BOX STEALING

FAVOURITE PASTIMES: CHASING SHEEP AND
EATING LEFTOVER PIZZA FROM THE WOOD OVEN

PET HATE: BIRDS
OBSESSION: FOOD
NAUGHTIEST DEED: ROLLING IN ANYTHING SMELLY
FAVOURITE PASTIME: CHASING SEAGULLS AT THE BEACH

PETER

OWNER: BRIONI OLIVER | SPRINGER SPANIEL X, 16 | **OLIVER'S TARANGA** McLAREN VALE, SA | 131

BECKY

PET HATE: NOT GETTING ENOUGH FOOD
FAVOURITE FOOD: CUSTOMERS' PICNICS
OBSESSION: FOOD, FOOD AND MORE FOOD
FAVOURITE PASTIME: HELPING HARVEST GRAPES
KNOWN ACCOMPLICES: JASPER AND PIPPIN THE CAT
NAUGHTIEST DEED: ROLLING IN DEAD KANGAROO CARCASSES

HAY SHED HILL WILYABRUP, WA | LABRADOODLE, 2 | OWNER: MICHAEL KERRIGAN

GIACOMO 'JACK' AKA FABIO

FAVOURITE FOOD: PÂTÉ ON TOAST
OBSESSIONS: PÂTÉ AND SCHMACKOS
PET HATES: SCOOTERS AND SKATEBOARDS
NAUGHTIEST DEED: CHEWING ACCESSORIES
KNOWN ACCOMPLICES: ARCHIE AND MATILDA
FAVOURITE TOYS: BROWN BEAR AND ARCHIE'S TOY CARS

OWNER: CHLOE EARL | DACHSHUND, 6 | **BROWN BROTHERS MILAWA VINEYARD** MILAWA, VIC

133

PET HATE: SNAKES
FAVOURITE TOY: HIS FOOTY
FAVOURITE FOOD: STAFF LUNCHES
FAVOURITE PASTIME: CHASING SWALLOWS IN THE WINERY
NAUGHTIEST DEED: EATING THE 3-PHASE REFRIGERATION CABLES
OBSESSION: DOING A VICTORY DANCE EVERY TIME A BOX OF WINE GOES OUT THE DOOR

WARRABILLA WINES RUTHERGLEN, VIC │ RED HEELER, 16 │ OWNER: ANDREW SMITH

MONTY

FAVOURITE TOY: BALL
PET HATES: THUNDER AND LIGHTNING
OBSESSION: CHASING BALLS AND RABBITS
NAUGHTIEST DEED: CHEWING UP VIV'S BEST SHOES
FAVOURITE PASTIMES: CHASING A BALL AND SLEEPING IN THE SUN

PET HATE: GOING IN THE CAR
NAUGHTIEST DEED: BREAKING A
WINDOW WHILE CHASING THE BALL
FAVOURITE FOOD: ROAST PORK CRACKLING
FAVOURITE PASTIME: GREETING CUSTOMERS
IN THE HOPE OF A BALL BEING THROWN

BAZ

OBSESSION: SPOTS
KNOWN ACCOMPLICE: ALWAYS MAX
PET HATE: HYDROHOUND, THE DOG WASHER
FAVOURITE FOOD: ANYTHING SILVER SERVICE
FAVOURITE PASTIME: BEING IN CHARGE OF GUEST RELATIONS
NAUGHTIEST DEED: HIDING UNDER HELEN'S DESK WHEN SHE IS WET

FINN

OBSESSION: RABBITS
FAVOURITE TOY: FINN'S TAIL
KNOWN ACCOMPLICE: ALWAYS FINN
FAVOURITE FOOD: ANYTHING HELEN EATS
PET HATE: OTHER DOGS ON HER VERANDAH
FAVOURITE PASTIME: VINEYARD SUPERVISION
NAUGHTIEST DEED: ROLLING IN SEAMUNGUS FERTILISER

MAX

MADISON D. DOG

NAUGHTIEST DEED: OIL PAINT PAWS
PET HATE: SHARING FOOD WITH JACK THE CAT
OBSESSION: BEING FIRST TO THE FRONT SEAT IN THE CAR
FAVOURITE TOY: COLOUR AND MOVEMENT, IE JACK THE CAT
FAVOURITE PASTIME: PRANCING ON THE BEACH AT PORT WILLUNGA
FAVOURITE FOOD: WHAT FOOD? I HAVEN'T BEEN FED. NO ONE HAS FED ME FOR AGES
OBSESSIONS: SERIOUSLY, WHAT FOOD, WHERE? LOOK AT ME. I'M STARVING

Looking for a break from the old cold kennel this holiday season?

Why not get off the leash, loosen the collar, jump in the back seat, wind the window down (oops, not that much!) let your tongue hang out and head to McLaren Vale on the Fleurieu Peninsula. Book a BB & BB (just call the McLaren Vale Bean Bag & Breakfast Bones Association) put up your paws, and become the pampered pooch that you were born to be.

STORY BY FOOD & WINE CORRESPONDENT: MADISON D. DOG

THE LURE OF WALKIES on the beach and barking at winery dogs at some of Australia's finest winery cellar doors has its attractions, but when it's all said and done, treats aren't treats without treats.

From show pup pedigree to runt of the litter, McLaren Vale is a Dog's paradise. But it hasn't always been so, things have certainly changed here over the years. When Melbourne and Australia's foremost canine *bon vivant* and critic, Riley Ace of Dogs, first wrote of a visit to McLaren Vale in the early 1960s, a cold pie and stale lamington from the bakery was the height of gastronomy, a dog's dinner indeed!

A ham bone round the back of Hamlets Smokehouse on the main street of Willunga was, and still is the best in the country, but sophisticated doggie dining was yet to mark its territory in McLaren Vale.

Riley's bark was always worse than his bite, and the 120-dog-year-old Murchison Terrier is now amazed at the range of world-class dog-friendly venues in the district today. It all began with the Barn restaurant and gallery in 1970 on the main street of McLaren Vale and now it seems every dog and his man has a place to pull up a bowl and enjoy the delights of the region.

My host for the week was the gregarious, gangly and somewhat unkempt Caribbean setter, Pascoe from Samuel's Gorge Winery, who led me through the best smells the region has to offer. We lifted a leg or two together on winery rubbish bins and dined outside some of Australia's finest restaurants.

Here's my pick of the best half-dozen but there are plenty more to sniff out.

d'Arry's Verandah
OSBORN ROAD, McLAREN VALE

Perched above the townships of McLaren Vale with great views to the ocean and Port Willunga, and if you are a water dog your host Coco, a feisty four-year-old golden retriever who is more than happy to take you over to the dam for a dip, and if the dam is dry there is always d'Arry Osborn's original swimming pool to cool down in before lunch.

d'Arry's Verandah restaurant not only deserves its worldwide reputation for a decade of excellence but also is set amongst kangaroo-filled scrub with rabbits galore. Need I say more?

Fino
HILL STREET, WILLUNGA

In the heart of charming Willunga, Fino is primarily a pussy-friendly venue but mutts are also welcome. The kitchen garden is a great place to wait for some Iberian-inspired dishes that all incorporate the best local ingredients. Tapas with a twist. Sophisticated dining indeed. Have your leash hitched to the picket fence out the front on a Saturday morning, and watch the fur pass by for the weekly Willunga produce markets. Country-killed local lamb and beef are the highlights. Then stay for lunch for an über-sophisticated but still authentic McLaren Vale meal. City meets country in style.

Russell's

HIGH STREET, WILLUNGA

A legendary McLaren Vale eatery, wood oven restaurant and anthropological experiment. The best table is by the back door of the kitchen between the wood oven and fire pit. You will be amazed at how many pats a dog from out of town can get sitting here.

Thankfully cutlery and crockery are pretty much absent at Russell's, so just wolf down the amazing wood oven pizzas from wooden boards and watch myriad locals, (hundreds each Friday and Saturday nights) pass by; from grape farmers, hippies, cyclists, artists and just plain old leash leaders. Each white ute in the line-up outside waiting for take-away will have a wine dog on board, so making friends with the locals is easy work here.

Salopian Inn

CNR McMURTRIE AND WILLUNGA ROADS, McLAREN VALE

A long-time Wine Dogs favourite. The Salopian Inn has a special place in the gastronomic history of the region and is a great place to visit. Sitting under the old fig tree or on the cool of the 1850s slate veranda overlooking the vineyards is a must for any visiting canine. The famous Salopian Inn McLaren Vale Shiraz pie is a classic dish that has everything you could wish for on the one plate.

Recommended by the black curly-coated retriever 'Benson' at the Gourmet Retreat, this place lives up to its reputation, no bones about it.

Victory Hotel

MAIN SOUTH ROAD, SELLICKS BEACH

Your hosts are the rambunctious Boris and Swahili, seven and forty-two in dog years. Well-bred but badly behaved, these much-loved golden retrievers are the publican's dogs that not only meet and greet, but meat and Greek. A great grill, fresh local seafood and serious cellar are topped off with hilltop views of the Mount Lofty ranges falling into the Gulf of St Vincent, the patron saint of Wine Dogs.

A stonewall-enclosed lawn and specimen gum tree and flag pole at one end for relief is magic. Watching the sun set over the Gulf with a lamb bone in the bowl, I can't help but think "Who's a good dog then? You're a good dog. Good dog!"

Star of Greece

THE ESPLANADE, PORT WILLUNGA

This place was recommended highly by Pascoe my Rastafarian guide and wow, what a place. The Star of Greece is a classic Australian seaside café but it is also a serious restaurant. Your host is Max, a little white West Highland-Maltese cross with a dash of poodle. He is so charming and unaffected and is the epitome of a restaurant dog. Meet and greet is Max's speciality.

Sitting on the cliff-top overlooking the silver sands of Port Willunga beach and the glistening gulf is something to bark about. However, the location combined with fishermen's bait AND Frisbees everywhere, this is living the dream. Sublime squid caught off the beach, cooked on the spot cannot be beaten and the occasional dropped ice-cream to be licked off the ground at the cafe outside is dessert as good as it gets. This is where McLaren Vale's sea and vines do actually come together.

Kitchen Door at Penny's Hill Winery

MAIN ROAD, McLAREN VALE

A dog's paradise run by a cat! Who would have thought, but pioneering ex-State premier Don Dunstan's legacy lives on. Your host, known as 'Chook Cat' was born on site in the ancient gum tree in the 1850s era chook house and meets and greets all and sundry outside the cellar door. But be warned Chook Cat is no kitten when it comes to any provocative sniffing, so expect a scratch or two if you are out of line.

Sitting amongst the vines, a classic Australian farm house and striking galvanized iron winery and restaurant, being at the Kitchen Door is the perfect spot for any dog. Despite the extraordinary highlights of the ever-changing and critically acclaimed local seasonal menu, the air-dried, super-marbled, 40-day-old Coorong Angus Beef fillet is the highlight of our trip. Dippy Dogs it ain't, this is a 'not to be missed' restaurant in the heart of McLaren Vale's vineyards.

THIS GUIDE WAS AS BARKED BY **MADISON D. DOG**, A FOUR-YEAR-OLD RIDGEBACK, TO ELENA AND ZAR BROOKS. ELENA HAS BEEN A WINEMAKER IN McLAREN VALE FOR A DECADE AND IS NOW MAKING WINE FOR HER OWN WINERY, DANDELION VINEYARDS, AND THE LATTER IS HER HUSBAND AND TYPIST WHO, ON OCCASION, IS ALLOWED A TASTE, ONLY OF COURSE, IF HE IS A GOOD BOY.

PET HATE: *STRAY DOGS*
FAVOURITE TOY: *OTHER DOGS' COLLARS*
OBSESSION: *RUNNING IN THE VINEYARD*
KNOWN ACCOMPLICES: *ELLA AND TAL ARBEL*
NAUGHTIEST DEED: *BRINGING ROADKILL HOME*
FAVOURITE PASTIME: *RIDING ON THE FORKLIFT AND FOUR-WHEELER*
FAVOURITE FOODS: *DRY FOOD, CHICKEN AND ANYTHING THAT FALLS OFF THE TABLE*

POLLYANNA

TESS

OBSESSION: *TENNIS BALL*
FAVOURITE TOY: *TENNIS BALL*
KNOWN ACCOMPLICE: *RALPH*
FAVOURITE PASTIME: *SLEEPING*
FAVOURITE FOOD: *SOMETHING SOFT*
PET HATE: *RUBY THE NEIGHBOUR'S KELPIE*

PET HATE: FLIES
OBSESSION: THE UTE
FAVOURITE FOOD: RABBIT
FAVOURITE PASTIME: RUNNING
KNOWN ACCOMPLICE: HIS BROTHER KOBER
NAUGHTIEST DEED: PEEING ON A CUSTOMER
FAVOURITE TOYS: ROPE RAG AND TENNIS BALLS

RALPH

SHADOW

FAVOURITE TOY: BALL
PET HATE: FLUFFY MAX THE CAT
OBSESSION: CHEWING SOFT TOYS
KNOWN ACCOMPLICE: FLUFFY MAX THE CAT
FAVOURITE FOODS: LIVER TREATS AND SWEET BISCUITS
FAVOURITE PASTIMES: SLEEPING AND COMING TO THE WINERY
NAUGHTIEST DEEDS: EATING DAVID'S BOOTS AND CHEWING THE FURNITURE

PET HATE: GETTING STUNG BY A BEE
OBSESSIONS: MAGPIES, BLOWIES AND BEES
FAVOURITE TOY: ANY HARD FRUIT OR WALNUTS
KNOWN ACCOMPLICES: RUSTY AND MAX THE CAT
NAUGHTIEST DEEDS: DIGGING HOLES AND CHEWING BOOTS
FAVOURITE PASTIMES: GREETING VISITORS AND HERDING MAGPIES

ROXY

MADDIE

PET HATE: *PHOTOGRAPHERS*
FAVOURITE PASTIME: *GARDENING*
NAUGHTIEST DEED: *TAKING OFF WITH
HER BOYFRIEND FOR A COUPLE OF DAYS*
OBSESSIONS: *MICE, KANGAROOS, POSSUMS
AND ANYTHING THAT MOVES IN THE NIGHT*

| **PAXTON** McLAREN VALE, SA | FOX TERRIER X 4 | OWNER: BEN PAXTON

PET HATE: RATSACK
FAVOURITE FOOD: CHOCOLATE
OBSESSIONS: POSSUMS AND CATS
FAVOURITE PASTIME: LYING ON A CUSHION
IN THE SUN AND GETTING A TUMMY RUB
NAUGHTIEST DEED: EATING RATSACK (SIX TIMES)

MADGE

OWNER: BEN PAXTON | JACK RUSSELL TERRIER X, 13 | **PAXTON** McLAREN VALE, SA | 147

MAX

FAVOURITE TOY: FRISBEE
PET HATE: DIESEL TRUCKS
OBSESSION: HAVING SOMEONE THROW A TOY
FAVOURITE FOOD: HOME-COOKED CHICKEN AND RICE
FAVOURITE PASTIME: CHEWING STICKS INTO TINY PIECES
NAUGHTIEST DEED: PRETENDING TO BE A TOUGH GUARD DOG

MERLOT

FAVOURITE PASTIME:
CUDDLING PEOPLE WITH HIS
TONGUE SLIGHTLY POKING OUT
NAUGHTIEST DEED: CUTTING POWER TO THE
HOUSE WHILE CHEWING EXTENSION CORD TWICE
PET HATE: BEING TOLD OFF – HE'S A SENSITIVE LAD
OBSESSION: BITING MAX'S HEELS WHILE MAX CHASES THE FRISBEE

CREED OF BAROSSA LYNDOCH, SA │ BORDER COLLIE, 6 AND KELPIE X, 3 │ OWNERS: MARK AND MANDY CREED

OBSESSION: BARREL BUNGS
FAVOURITE TOY: BARREL BUNG
PET HATE: ELECTRIC FENCES - OUCH!
KNOWN ACCOMPLICES: MAX AND MERLOT
FAVOURITE PASTIME: JUMPING IN AND OUT OF THE UTE
NAUGHTIEST DEED: CROSSING ROADS WITHOUT LOOKING

JACKY

OWNERS: DANIEL AND TARNYA EGGLETON | COOLIE X ? | *CREED OF BAROSSA* LYNDOCH SA | 149

KOBER

PET HATE: SCARY PEOPLE
KNOWN ACCOMPLICES: RALPH AND PANCHO
FAVOURITE PASTIMES: STARING AT THE CHOOK
PEN AND RUNNING IN FRONT OF THE UTE
FAVOURITE FOODS: CHICKEN AND LEFTOVERS
OBSESSIONS: TENNIS BALLS AND THE CHOOK PEN
NAUGHTIEST DEED: RUNNING 42KM TO PLAY WITH HIS BROTHER RALPH

OBSESSION: FOOD
FAVOURITE TOY: MARK'S SOCKS
KNOWN ACCOMPLICES: RODNEY AND JIM JIM
NAUGHTIEST DEED: PINCHING MARY'S SLIPPERS
FAVOURITE PASTIME: CAR JOURNEYS; SITTING BETWEEN
THE TWO FRONT SEATS, WATCHING THE WORLD GO BY
PET HATE: BEING LEFT OUT OF FAMILY ADVENTURES

HORACE

FAVOURITE TOY: HIS WALKING LEAD
PET HATE: BEING LEFT HOME ALONE
OBSESSION: CELLAR DOOR AND OFFICE STAFF
NAUGHTIEST DEED: COMING TO WORK ON HIS OWN
FAVOURITE FOOD: ANYTHING THAT PEOPLE ARE EATING
FAVOURITE PASTIME: COMING TO WORK (AT EVERY OPPORTUNITY)
KNOWN ACCOMPLICES: ALL THE FEMALE STAFF AT SEPPELTSFIELD

FERDIE

MALBEC

FAVOURITE TOY: BUNGS
PET HATE: PINOT NOIR
OBSESSIONS: SLEEPING IN DOMINIQUE'S
BRIEFCASE AND DIGGING UP THE POT PLANTS
NAUGHTIEST DEED: PLAYING MATADOR WITH THE COWS
KNOWN ACCOMPLICES: THE GARDENER AND EX-POLICEMAN GEOFF

PET HATE: BEING STILL
KNOWN ACCOMPLICE: HARRY
FAVOURITE FOOD: STEAK LEFTOVERS
FAVOURITE TOY: HARRY THE LABRADOR
NAUGHTIEST DEED: JUMPING THE FENCE TO
JUMP UP ON STRANGERS AT THE RESTAURANT
FAVOURITE PASTIMES: RUNNING AND JUMPING FENCES

PINOT

PORTIA

*FAVOURITE PASTIME: SPENDING
TIME INSIDE WITH THE FAMILY*
*FAVOURITE FOOD: POACHED EGGS
LEFT OVER FROM THE GIRLS' BREAKFASTS*
PET HATE: GOING TO THE DOG KENNEL
OBSESSION: FOLLOWING SAM AROUND THE WINERY

PET HATE: DIESEL CARS
FAVOURITE FOOD: MINCE
KNOWN ACCOMPLICES: LUIS AND PORTIA
FAVOURITE PASTIME: FOLLOWING LUIS AROUND
OBSESSIONS: CHASING COWS AND KEEPING SNAKES AWAY
FROM ARABELLA, CATERINA AND ALLEGRA IN SUMMER
NAUGHTIEST DEED: EATING ARABELLA, CATERINA AND ALLEGRA'S BARBIE DOLLS

FREDDIE

OWNER: SAM MIRANDA

OBSESSION: STICKS
PET HATE: DIESEL CARS
KNOWN ACCOMPLICES: PORTIA AND FRED
FAVOURITE FOOD: DOG BONES FROM THE LOCAL BUTCHER
FAVOURITE PASTIME: CHASING STICKS AROUND THE VINEYARD
NAUGHTIEST DEED: LEAVING WET STICKS AROUND THE HOUSE

LUIS

OBSESSION: CHEWING BARK OFF THE FIG TREE
PET HATE: BEING OUTSIDE IN THE COLD
NAUGHTIEST DEED: STEALING SUGAR
STICKS FROM CAFE TABLES
FAVOURITE TOY: VINE CLIPPINGS
FAVOURITE PASTIME: GETTING UP
AND GOING BACK TO BED

ALFALFA

TAYLOR

FAVOURITE FOOD: CHICKEN
PET HATE: BIRDS ON THE VINES
KNOWN ACCOMPLICE: SHADOW
FAVOURITE PASTIMES: SWIMMING,
EATING PRUNINGS AND CHASING BIRDS
NAUGHTIEST DEED: CHASING CHICKENS
OBSESSION: CATCHING SILVEREYES UNDER THE NETS

OBSESSION: BABIES
FAVOURITE TOY: JASON
FAVOURITE PASTIME: SLEEPING
KNOWN ACCOMPLICES: RABBITS
PET HATE: NOT BEING FED ON TIME (6.15PM)
NAUGHTIEST DEED: DIGGING A MONSTER HOLE IN THE LAWN

GUS

OWNERS: KEVIN

PEBBLES

PET HATE: FLIES
FAVOURITE TOY: COLIN
NAUGHTIEST DEED: THE PLOVER INCIDENT
FAVOURITE FOOD: CELLAR DOOR LEFTOVERS
FAVOURITE PASTIME: RIDING ON THE FLAT-TRAY
OBSESSION: CHASING RABBITS AND FIELD MICE
KNOWN ACCOMPLICES: CASPER AND COLIN

PET HATE: MYNAH BIRDS
FAVOURITE FOOD: MEAT BONES
FAVOURITE TOYS: BALLS AND STICKS
KNOWN ACCOMPLICES: WILBUR AND LUCY
OBSESSION: PLAYING WITH SHELLS ON THE BEACH
FAVOURITE PASTIMES: SWIMMING, SURFING AND RETRIEVING
NAUGHTIEST DEED: EATING THE CHEESE PLATTER AT A DINNER PARTY

MOLLY

XENA

PET HATE: BEING EXCLUDED
FAVOURITE FOOD: HUMAN FOOD
OBSESSION: ESCAPING FROM THE BACKYARD
NAUGHTIEST DEED: DIGGING TUNNELS UNDER THE GATE
FAVOURITE TOYS: ANY SMALL, PASSING RABBIT, BIRD, LIZARD...
FAVOURITE PASTIMES: HANGING OUT AT THE CELLAR DOOR AND SINGING

KNOWN ACCOMPLICE: SPLASH
FAVOURITE FOOD: SLOW-COOKED BEEF
OBSESSIONS: BIRDS, BARBECUES AND BEES
FAVOURITE PASTIME: GREETING CELLAR DOOR
CUSTOMERS, PARTICULARLY THOSE WITH FOOD
PET HATES: BEING WASHED AND TRIPS TO THE VET
NAUGHTIEST DEED: HELPING HERSELF TO THE MARINATING BEEF

DHARMA

MAX

FAVOURITE PASTIME: SLEEPING
OBSESSION: CUDDLING WITH KIDS
PET HATE: NOT GETTING ATTENTION
KNOWN ACCOMPLICES: CHLOE, KADE AND GEORGIA
NAUGHTIEST DEED: SNEAKING INTO WARM SPOTS FOR A SLEEP

FAVOURITE TOY: MAX
NAUGHTIEST DEED: CHASING RABBITS
AND KANGAROOS IN THE VINEYARD
KNOWN ACCOMPLICES: CHLOE, KADE AND GEORGIA
FAVOURITE PASTIME: CHEWING THINGS HE SHOULDN'T
OBSESSIONS: PLAYING WITH MAX AND BITING HIS EARS

SAM

OBSESSION: PEOPLE
FAVOURITE TOY: BARNEY THE BEAR
PET HATE: BEING TAUNTED BY THE INDOOR CAT
KNOWN ACCOMPLICE: DEXTER FROM TEMPUS TWO
FAVOURITE PASTIME: CHASING STARLINGS AND SWALLOWS
NAUGHTIEST DEED: CHEWING A PAIR OF SASS AND BIDE JEANS
FAVOURITE FOOD: ANYTHING WITH BONES AND A DECENT STENCH

WOODY

WYATT

OBSESSION: FOOD
PET HATE: HAVING A BATH
FAVOURITE FOOD: PETE'S PIZZA
NAUGHTIEST DEED: JUMPING OUT
THE WINDOW OF A MOVING CAR
KNOWN ACCOMPLICES: BELLA AND TOBY
FAVOURITE TOY: MELINDA'S SHIRT SLEEVE

FAVOURITE FOOD: YO-YO BISCUITS
NAUGHTIEST DEED: DIGGING HOLES
IN THE LAWN PRIOR TO A WEDDING
OBSESSION: EYEING OFF THE HORSES
FAVOURITE TOY: TRISTAN'S SOCCER BALL
FAVOURITE PASTIME: MONITORING THE VINES WITH ROZ

BELLA

OBSESSION: EATING
FAVOURITE TOY: FOOD
FAVOURITE PASTIME: EATING
FAVOURITE FOOD: PETE'S PIZZA
KNOWN ACCOMPLICES: WYATT AND BELLA
NAUGHTIEST DEED: EATING 20KGS OF DRY DOG FOOD

TOBY

HAMISH

PET HATE: SKATEBOARDS

FAVOURITE PASTIME: BEING A CELEBRITY
BY HAVING HIS OWN CHARDONNAY LABEL

KNOWN ACCOMPLICES: BEAR AND SASCHA

NAUGHTIEST DEED: DIGGING UP BEAR'S BONES

OBSESSION: TRYING TO FIT DOWN RABBIT-HOLES

GUN FOR HIRE

by Zoe Williams

I WAS POSSESSED by a certain amount of festering resentment, as I travelled up to visit my parents, although I never discussed any of this with the dog. The dog, I will admit, was poorly trained. He was not trained at all. We had lived in the city all his life, and if we're going to date my life from when I got the point of it at all, all mine too. People in the city don't train their dogs, they just pick up their – what do they call it in training, "business" – and hope for the best.

So, anyway. I don't want you to think I'd been burdening the dog, nor that I was one of those men who tries to reason with his dog, conversationally, in subconscious preparation for the day he accepts that only a creature bought-and-paid-for will ever suffer his company.

No.

And I don't, furthermore, think that he would have sniffed out my grievances, wordlessly. He isn't that kind of dog. These animals can be remarkable, I don't doubt – I met a Swedish guy once, whose Boxer could say "mama". I read a story about a Pekinese who correctly diagnosed his owner's breast cancer by repeatedly barking at her breasts (you have to take your hat off to her, as well, though – a lesser owner might not think "I'll have a mammogram", she might think "for God's sake, dog! We're meant to be in this together!") And I also met a schnauzer when I was a kid who could yodel 'Old MacDonald Had a Farm', but childhood memories are just one long land-mined pass of adult lies. There was probably a guy hiding in a bush somewhere with a tape of dog-yodelling.

Mine is not a remarkable dog. Honestly? His intellect, as it ranks in his species set, reminds me of my own. No bells and whistles, but he will work out what he needs to know, fractionally before he needs to know it.

I certainly never noticed any tension or discomfort in him, as we travelled back home, even though I was practising, as I always am, a line that I will never pursue, to silence my mother who will never be silenced. "Do you never wonder, mother..." (in fact, I call her "mummy". But I hate the fact that I've never been able to drop the "mummy", so I never call her anything at all. When I want to get her attention or be emphatic, I just shuffle into a more noticeable/forceful area of the room)... "Does it never occur to you, mummy..." (it annoys me that I'm trying to be authentic in a practice-argument that I will 100 per cent never have the guts to have) "why I don't make these personal remarks to you? Do you think it's because I think you are running your life perfectly, that you look perfect and all your decisions are perfect? Do you think this is at all likely? Or do you think maybe I'm being tactful? Is there any chance you might exercise some tact towards me?" This fake fight was unsatisfactory, not cataclysmic enough to warrant practising, though of course, much too dramatic, much too cataclysmic, for me to ever say out loud. God forbid. That I should ever say a tetchy but essentially rather minor thing, instead of sitting here, festering...

Instead of that, I directed my psyche to a fake argument I was having with my father, a more complicated imaginative task since it relied on his uttering something true, something he thought, before it could start. He would have to say that he thought I was going nowhere. He would have to come out and call me a loser. Just say it. "You loser. Whatever flimflam you're working on, loser, that isn't work, that's just city bullshit. Whatever you think you're making, loser, you're not making a family of your own, there probably is no better use for you than coming back to tend to the people who gave you life, considering the many thousands of dollars we've given you as well... Loser." He would have to say all that, and he never would. My mother, conversely, can always be relied on to make an unpleasant personal remark. She is the rising sun of the small-scale insult. She will survive the apocalypse and wake up with a querulous "why are you so pale? Are you on drugs?"

Worrying away, driving with the wheel in one hand and the dog's ear in the other, trying to make my imaginary-father say something revealing so I could irrupt. Something simple: "Is there any point to your work, or are you, as I suspect, a glorified administrative assistant in a company that thinks it fashionable to like losers?" Yeah... in fairness, I'm not sure he even thinks that. It's not my job specifically he disrespects, it's all jobs that aren't his job.

The dog had started to pant, foam, even, as the heat in the car intensified, and this lent him a geriatric aspect that I think threw me off guard. Not that I had ever been on guard with the dog, I mean. But the truth of it was, I wasn't really paying any attention to him, just wiping his drool off my neck without thinking, as I drew closer to my roots and felt progressively worse. I don't see how they could expect me to stay here. If you can't love a place as beautiful as this, then you were born not to love it. There's nothing to be done, you can't cajole someone into a sensitivity for this scenery. I do not have that kind of poetry in my soul, I have no affinity with the land. But I'm not blind, I'm not a fool; I was just meant for a different kind of place, away from these neat rows and productivity, away from this perfect meeting of man and nature, I prefer a place with chaos, where sometimes – often – productivity doesn't seem to be the point. I do not think I said any of this out loud to the dog. Nothing changed in his demeanour. I'd turned the stereo off, thinking perhaps that the jaunty aggression of the music was furnacing my mood. We were nearly there, and as I pictured that fake welcome of the way they stood upon the porch, apparently disappointed, I always thought, to find me on the path, as if it were an act of characteristic laziness and perversity that I wasn't already in the house.

"Son! Still useless, son? Still can't park, son? Still got that shit car?"

In fairness, I couldn't really hear him; I could just see him waving. I was parking pretty badly, because the dog was whinnying lawlessly at the window, and it was distracting. He's not a small dog. I was thinking, if he's going to behave like this, I might as well keep a horse. But still I didn't put his lead on, because he is not the kind of dog who needs that kind of precaution.

"Hello, Love. You've..." she started off bold, herself. Very quickly, although it plays quite slowly in my mind, her tone took a new and I have to say pretty unusual direction. "Is he..? Is he ok..?" The dog was bounding toward her, and she was right, there was something unfriendly about him, though I can't tell you what it was. He wasn't barking or anything. I'm not stupid. He was just moving a little too fast.

"He's fine…" I said irritably, and here the whole thing shames me, really. I can see her turning, awkwardly, up the stairs, aiming back to the house. Her movements, her thick trunk and physical fear, all impeding grace and, more to the point, speed, so that the dog was upon her before she'd even got a decent foothold on the top step. My dad was only a yard in front of her, but he was just sputtering and flapping. The dog by now had the bottom of her trouser leg, and made pretty short work of that, so that soon she had, like, a hoola-skirt of savaged slacks. Violence against the person, though, did not seem to be his game, or not in the immediate term. Having shown he meant business, he barked her along the porch, until she had climbed onto the swing seat and was crouched there. Dad rushed him from behind, trying to grab his collar, but the dog turned as he lurched forward, growling and now frothing. My dad lost his balance, and pitched towards my mother, who drew him only the seat, which shook and creaked as it swung, now, with the weight of the pair of them, half-standing. "Get away! Away". My dad was shouting pretty loud, so I can't say what my mother was shouting, though I should imagine she had something to say about it.

And I never moved. It was all so slow but, at the same time, so fast. As suddenly as it had started, it stopped: the dog turned round and came bounding back to me, although this time there was no menace, his pace was exuberant. As he reached me, he leapt up to cannon me in the chest, which he has never done before. I can only describe him as triumphant. It's impossible to love a dog and not be moved by a display like that. I mean the triumph. Not the bit where he rounded up my parents.

I looked back to the swing seat, which they'd both disembarked; my dad was checking the swing mechanism, as if to make sure it could support any other half-standing old people who might take refuge on it in the future. My mom was staring at me, agape, and I'm ashamed, again, to say this annoyed me. She was hoping to convey outrage with her dropped jaw, and I was vexed that she returned to her normal, obnoxious personality so soon after a calamity. Also, if I'm honest, she suddenly looked 105, and I was frightened.

Well I was still right next to the car; the best thing I could think of to do was to get back into it. The dog leapt in beside me, good as gold, as incongruously tame as a circus animal. It sounds cowardly, but I didn't want to get into an argument, straight away, about whether it was the dog's fault. I thought I could return, maybe without the dog, and have that argument later.

On the way home, the dog sat placid, upright, in the front seat, apparently satisfied and at peace. It dawned on me that this idiot mutt thought we'd driven five hours, just to do that, and were now driving five hours home, job well done. And with all the awkward stuff ahead, and probably another five hours in the car tomorrow, I have to admit, this made me smile.

ZOE WILLIAMS IS A COLUMNIST FOR *THE GUARDIAN*, ALONG WITH SUNDRY OTHER ENGLISH PUBLICATIONS AND THE ODD IN-FLIGHT MAGAZINE. SHE HAS A STAFFIE-RIDGEBACK CROSS CALLED SPOT; AS YET, NO VINEYARD.

MAAIKE BERNS

OBSESSION: CHASING BIRDS
FAVOURITE FOOD: TRUFFLE OMELETTE
KNOWN ACCOMPLICES: ALLIE, ERROL,
SHAYNE, DIGIT, ROXY AND SKYE
FAVOURITE TOY: EVERLASTING FIRE PLUG
NAUGHTIEST DEED: SNEAKING INTO THE CAFÉ
PET HATE: BEING LEFT OUT OF TRUFFLE HUNTS

CHILLI

BUNDY

PET HATES: WAVES AND THUNDER
FAVOURITE TOY: RUBBER THONGS
KNOWN ACCOMPLICES: SAM AND JED
FAVOURITE PASTIME: LONG WALKS ON THE BEACH
OBSESSION: ROLLING IN THE SAND AFTER A SWIM
NAUGHTIEST DEED: BURYING ONE SHOE OF A PAIR

FAVOURITE TOY: SQUEAKY TOY
OBSESSION: ANYTHING THAT MOVES
KNOWN ACCOMPLICES: BUNDY AND JED
NAUGHTIEST DEED: DIGGING IN THE FERN GARDEN ON HOT DAYS
FAVOURITE PASTIMES: SWIMMING AND RUNNING AT THE BEACH

SAM

ROSE MARIE

OBSESSION: THE CAT
FAVOURITE FOOD: CURRY
PET HATE: PUTTING HER COLLAR ON
FAVOURITE PASTIME: CHASING HARPER
FAVOURITE TOY: CHILDREN'S POSSESSIONS
KNOWN ACCOMPLICE: CORDY MOUSE THE CAT
NAUGHTIEST DEED: EATING "THE BOOK OF TASHI"

PET HATE: THUNDER
OBSESSION: RABBITS
KNOWN ACCOMPLICE: SAM
FAVOURITE FOOD: KANGAROO
FAVOURITE TOY: TREE BRANCHES
FAVOURITE PASTIMES: EATING AND SLEEPING
NAUGHTIEST DEED: PINCHING STRAWBERRIES AND AVOCADOS FROM THE GARDEN

RALPH

JACKSON

PET HATE: TAKING ORDERS
FAVOURITE TOY: NEW, EXPENSIVE,
CHEWY BARREL BUNGS THAT BOUNCE
OBSESSION: UNIDENTIFIED FLYING OBJECTS
FAVOURITE PASTIME: RIDING "SHOTGUN" IN THE UTE
NAUGHTIEST DEED: USING CHOOK FEATHERS AS DENTAL FLOSS

IN MEMORY OF

STEVE IRWIN

"THE CROCODILE HUNT

KNOWN ACCOMPLICE: MAGGIE
OBSESSION: EATING ALL THE KIDS' TOYS
PET HATE: BEING TOLD TO STAY AT HOME
NAUGHTIEST DEED: EATING ALL THE KIDS' TOYS
FAVOURITE FOODS: MEAT AND THE ODD MARRON
FAVOURITE PASTIMES: SLEEPING AND CHASING RABBITS

ZAC

KOLA

FAVOURITE TOY:
THE BUILDER'S SANDPILE

FAVOURITE FOOD: NANA KAY'S SHORTBREAD

FAVOURITE PASTIME: SLEEPING UNDER RESTAURANT
TABLES WHEN SHE IS SUPPOSED TO BE TIED UP

NAUGHTIEST DEED: FLATTENING THE BUILDER'S SANDPILE

OBSESSION: ESCAPING TO SEE WHAT THE GUESTS ARE EATING

OBSESSION: FOOD
FAVOURITE FOOD: GOAT
KNOWN ACCOMPLICES: BEAR, DENVER
AND WOLF, THE OTHER FARM DOGS
FAVOURITE PASTIMES: BURYING BONES AND
PLAYING WITH HIS FRIENDS ON THE FARM
NAUGHTIEST DEED: DIGGING UP THE VEGIE PATCH

TEDDY

CHELSEA

PET HATE: COWS
OBSESSION: HUNTING
FAVOURITE TOY: DEMETRIO
FAVOURITE FOOD: FETTUCCINE
FAVOURITE PASTIME: HUNTING
NAUGHTIEST DEED: JUMPING UP AND DOWN
KNOWN ACCOMPLICES: THE OTHER POINTER SISTERS

JESSE

PET HATE: COWS
OBSESSION: HUNTING
FAVOURITE TOY: DEMETRIO
FAVOURITE FOOD: SPAGHETTI
FAVOURITE PASTIME: RETRIEVING QUAIL
NAUGHTIEST DEEDS: BARKING AND SINGING
KNOWN ACCOMPLICES: THE OTHER POINTER SISTERS

DIANA

PET HATE: COWS
FAVOURITE FOOD: LASAGNE
FAVOURITE PASTIME: HUNTING
OBSESSIONS: HARES AND FOXES
NAUGHTIEST DEED: CHASING THINGS
KNOWN ACCOMPLICES: THE OTHER POINTER SISTERS

SANGIO

OBSESSION: LICKING
KNOWN ACCOMPLICE: FERGUS
PET HATES: PLANES AND THUNDER
FAVOURITE PASTIME: PRUNING WITH ALL HIS FRIENDS
NAUGHTIEST DEED: CONSUMING THE FAT FROM 2KG
OF PORCHETTA (ON A DRIP AT THE VET'S FOR 3 DAYS)
FAVOURITE TOY: NEW TENNIS BALLS (DOESN'T LIKE OLD ONES)

188   **TOTINO ESTATE** PARACOMBE SA | BORDER COLLIE 3 | OWNERS: DAMIEN HARRIS AND TORY SHEPHERD

NECTAR OF THE DOGS

by Tory Shepherd

DOGS AND VINEYARDS have a very genteel feel. Polished brown boots striding through neat rows, obedient dog at heel. Woodsmoke drifting softly over the rolling hills, gentling the crisp air. Tweed jackets, the glint of a fine red in a translucent glass, loyal hound keeping watch.

It's not quite like that up at our place, Totino Estate.

Everything looks picture-perfect. It's autumn in Paracombe and the leaves quickly turned red after harvest. The cover crop between the vines is bright green. A true Adelaide Hills autumn means the sky is almost painfully bright, a blue that sharply sets off the other colours.

And then there's Sangio. Again, on the surface, perfection.

Border collies are so, well, doggy. You see them on ads for dog food, vet shows, worming pills. Sangio (short for Sangiovese) has the distinctive white snout, collar, pelt and paws of his breed, contrasting neatly against shiny black. He has a sharp white tip on his tail, bright, inquisitive eyes, and an enormous tongue.

Border collies look smart and cool, an outdoors dog, born to herd and fetch.

Sangio has different talents.

Like many puppies, when he was small he wet himself when he got excited. It was funny at first, this little fur ball who was so happy to see you he just couldn't contain his excitement. It only became a bit of a concern when he was fully grown.

Visitors to the vineyard would eagerly greet the bounding bugger. He, in turn, would leap up – almost to shoulder height – just as he lost control of his bladder. Some, but not all, took it as the compliment it was meant to be.

He tries to help around the vineyard. He chases off the pesky birds and makes sure the sheep and alpacas are under control. He has taken it upon himself to chase airplanes and helicopters off the property. Whenever there's wine spilled in the shed, he's there to lick it up. He loves it – maybe too much. Every now and then, a cold wet snout will nudge someone's hand while they're holding a glass. It could be an accident, but the enthusiasm with which he licks up the spills is starting to make me suspicious. He is a glutton.

Once, in a feeding frenzy, he dug up every single bone he had ever buried, and ate them all. He looked very pleased with himself until the constipation kicked in. Thousands of dollars and several enemas later, we had a contrite and abashed dog with (according to the vet) "anal trauma". Delightful!

Shortly after, we threw a big party. Hundreds of people came and drank pinot and prosecco under the stars on a balmy evening. Sangio roamed around, nudging glasses and sucking up the spills. Everything was going swimmingly. Until someone noticed he had spent quite a bit of time on his back under the barbecue, sculling the fat as it drained out the back.

He was covered in the stuff, and by the next morning – despite our best efforts – he had a black halo of flies circling his head. But the worst was yet to come. He had drunk so much fat the vet could measure it in his bloodstream, and for three days he farted uncontrollably. Every time he stood up, every time he sat down.

When I was a kid, and the not-so-proud owner of a scrappy and balding mongrel called Neddy, all I wanted was a cool dog. A dog to show off to the other kids. It's taken me this long to realise that it's the bizarre, dorky behavior of our canine friends that makes them the best company, with no exceptions.

I'm a city chick who moved to the country with some trepidation. I still hate the earwigs and the millipedes, the spiders and the snakes. I kinda like the foxes and rabbits, although I'm not supposed to.

I had pictured this civilised existence, clean and crisp in the country air. What I got was a chaos of mud and crazy hours, leaks and freezing cold.

But what makes me love living here, on a vineyard, is the combination of wine and dogs.

There is a pure joy in sitting outside on the deck, overlooking the geometry of those vines with a glass in hand. I can close my eyes and feel the sun on my face and a refreshing breeze in my hair, as my dog nudges my wine onto the ground before running out to greet the next visitor. Perfect.

TORY SHEPHERD IS AN AWARD-WINNING JOURNALIST WITH A STACK OF DEGREES THAT DON'T ADD UP TO VERY MUCH. SHE LIVES WITH WINEMAKER/VITICULTURALIST AND HUSBAND-TO-BE DAMIEN HARRIS AND SANGIO AT TOTINO ESTATE.

OBSESSION: CROWS
KNOWN ACCOMPLICE: BONO
PET HATE: CROW NOISES AT 5 AM
FAVOURITE FOOD: ANY FOOD IN A TIN
FAVOURITE PASTIMES: ROLLING IN
COW PATS AND SMELLING FARM SMELLS
NAUGHTIEST DEEDS: CATCHING AN AILING
CHOOK AND SCARING A GUINEA FOWL TO DEATH

MICKY

OBSESSION: UTE RIDES
FAVOURITE TOY: FOOTBALL
KNOWN ACCOMPLICE: JANE
PET HATE: LACK OF ATTENTION
FAVOURITE PASTIME: TRICKS, ESPECIALLY HIGH FIVES
NAUGHTIEST DEED: SNEAKING IN AND SLEEPING ON THE COUCH

JESS

PET HATE: WALKING IN THE RAIN
OBSESSIONS: FOOD AND RABBITS
FAVOURITE TOY: SQUEAKY PLASTIC DOG
KNOWN ACCOMPLICE: HIS BROTHER BEN
FAVOURITE PASTIME: HUNTING FOR THINGS TO EAT
NAUGHTIEST DEED: EATING A WHOLE RABBIT, FUR AND ALL

BEAU

DIEGO

FAVOURITE FOOD: SHEEP
FAVOURITE TOY: TOY MONKEY
NAUGHTIEST DEED: ESCAPING
PET HATE: NOT BEING WALKED
OBSESSION: JUMPING ON PEOPLE
FAVOURITE PASTIME: EATING CHRISTMAS PUDDINGS

TARDY

PET HATE: EXERCISING
FAVOURITE FOOD: BONES
KNOWN ACCOMPLICE: DIEGO
FAVOURITE TOY: RUBBER CHICKEN
NAUGHTIEST DEED: EATING MEDICATION

FAVOURITE TOY: WOOLLY BLANKET
FAVOURITE FOOD: VEGEMITE SANDWICH
PET HATE: PEOPLE RAISING THEIR VOICES
FAVOURITE PASTIME: CHECKING OUT VISITORS'
CARS AND CHARDONNAY LODGE HAPPENINGS
OBSESSIONS: HER BASKET AND ANY BONE SHE HAS
NAUGHTIEST DEED: DIGGING UP THE LAWN TO EAT COCKCHAFER GRUBS

MEG

LEONARDIS

OBSESSIONS: THE CAT AND RABBIT
FAVOURITE FOOD: WALLABY SHANKS
FAVOURITE TOYS: THE CAT AND RABBIT
NAUGHTIEST DEED: LICKING THE CAT AND RABBIT
PET HATE: NOT BEING ABLE TO GET TO THE CAT AND RABBIT
KNOWN ACCOMPLICES: FLOSS THE CAT, BOBBY AND BUN BUNS THE RABBIT

PET HATE: MOTORBIKES
FAVOURITE FOOD: LAMB SHANKS
KNOWN ACCOMPLICES: BUSTER AND HUEY
OBSESSIONS: MOTORBIKES AND FORKLIFTS
NAUGHTIEST DEED: SWALLOWING FISH HOOKS
FAVOURITE TOYS: JULIAN'S SOCKS AND BARRELL BUNGS
FAVOURITE PASTIMES: CHASING BUNGS AND BARKING AT BIRDS

CHARLIE

POPPY

FAVOURITE FOOD: LAMB CHOPS
OBSESSION: BEING A BEACH CRICKET FIELDER
PET HATES: RUBY THE CAT AND HAVING A WASH
FAVOURITE PASTIME: RELAXING ON THE COUCH
FAVOURITE TOY: ANYTHING RESEMBLING A BALL
NAUGHTIEST DEED: EATING KIDS' LOW-LYING BREAKFASTS

OBSESSION: WATER
FAVOURITE FOOD: SCHMACKOS
PET HATES: CAMERAS AND BRIGHT LIGHTS
NAUGHTIEST DEED: BREAKING INTO HER FOOD
BOX AND EATING UNTIL SHE NEARLY EXPLODED
KNOWN ACCOMPLICES: PEDRO GARY AND BAXTER
FAVOURITE PASTIME: SWIMMING, SWIMMING, SWIMMING

HUDSON

HELGA

OBSESSION: BIRD CHASING
KNOWN ACCOMPLICE: FRIDA
FAVOURITE FOOD: CHICKEN NECKS
FAVOURITE TOY: HER SPECIAL RUG
NAUGHTIEST DEED: CHASING CARS
PET HATE: VALERIE'S GUINEA FOWLS
FAVOURITE PASTIME: LICKING UP SPILT BULLERS MUSCAT

FAVOURITE PASTIME: EATING
OBSESSION: CHASING RABBITS
PET HATE: HIGH PITCHED MUSIC
FAVOURITE FOOD: BULLERS MUSCAT
FAVOURITE TOY: VALERIE'S BEST FOOTWEAR
NAUGHTIEST DEED: EATING VALERIE'S SHOES

FRIDA

FAVOURITE TOY: CORKS
FAVOURITE FOOD: CHICKEN WINGS
NAUGHTIEST DEED: CHEWING SHOES
KNOWN ACCOMPLICES: TEDDY AND LILY
OBSESSION: 3PM IS CHICKY WING TIME
FAVOURITE PASTIME: PLAYING WITH RUDI
PET HATES: POPPING CORKS AND FIREWORKS

PERRI

ROLLING

PET HATE: THUNDER
FAVOURITE FOOD: STEAK
FAVOURITE TOY: GOLF BALLS
OBSESSION: CATCHING BOTTLE TOPS AND
HOLDING THEM ON THE TIP OF HIS TONGUE
NAUGHTIEST DEEDS: CHEWING IVAN'S FISHING
ROD AND NEIGHBOUR JOHN'S SUNGLASSES
KNOWN ACCOMPLICE: HIS LITTLE BROTHER MAXWELL

GEORDIE

TESS

PET HATE: THUNDER
KNOWN ACCOMPLICE: JESS
FAVOURITE TOY: PETER'S BOOTS
OBSESSIONS: FOOD, ATTENTION AND RABBITS
FAVOURITE PASTIMES: CHASING RABBITS AND LICKING PEOPLE
NAUGHTIEST DEED: DROPPING DEAD RABBITS AT THE BACK DOOR

DOG-DAY AFTERNOON

by Jason Hoy

I'VE SEEN A FEW DOGS IN MY TIME...

Stand behind the counter of any fine wine store on a Saturday morning and it's a regular Best in Show. The difference is the canines have all been let off the leash at the same time, are ravenous, and the only distraction available to the poor guy behind the counter is a collection of liquid-filled sticks. It's madness.

It's an incredibly high-pitched noise only discernible to the most sensitive ears: the whine of a corkscrew entering the cork of a good bottle of Burgundy for a free tasting around midday. They hear it from miles around. A pack mentality that will see the shop assistant mauled before the show even begins.

The first entrant is always somewhat of a bitzer, no particular breed, simply nervous and edgy and in desperate need to chase that car back down the road. The barking hangover. Once this parade has padded in and out with vinous bone in mouth, well, that's when the show really begins.

Look around the melee that surrounds the unfortunate shop assistant, bottle in hand, trickle of fear and sweat on their face and you'd guess it was simply a pack of wolves. The first five minutes is always the most brutal to watch. Like a pack of hyenas simultaneously attacking a nervous gazelle on the plain, many sinking into the sanguine-coloured offering on hand like it may be their last taste for months. Look a little closer and the breeds become a little more defined.

First to show themselves are the beagles. Incredible nose, incredibly intelligent, but what an appetite! Twenty wines are on offer but they can spot scents of Grand Cru, winemaking nobility, even high Parker points where most see nothing. And they are relentless in their pursuit. "Would you mind if I just had one more taste of that Chambertin?" or "Just another taste" or "One more sip of Musigny, please".

Then there are the fancy breeds: the poodles, chihuahuas, Bichon Frisé and Maltese terriers. All they smell is money. If the wine retailer can get their attention and lure them to a Champagne display, then they've got a friend for life, albeit a rather flighty self-absorbed one. Like all these breeds, don't pay them enough attention and you'll soon be on the receiving end of some annoying yip-yip-yipping and needle-like teeth. Their bark is far worse than their bite, quite unlike the next pack to descend on the tasting arena.

Your hunting dogs roam the store hungry to pick up the scent of that special bottle missing from their collection. Once they've picked it up, you can run through a forest of wines with a pack of bloodhounds, wolfhounds, coonhounds and Burghounds on your trail, wade through rivers of obscure appellations to try and throw them off, but they are relentless. The great thing about these breeds is they live for the thrill of the chase and are happy to share the spoils of the hunt with their companions. It all comes down to good breeding and training.

So it's mid-afternoon and the bottles are almost empty. Enter mischief and mayhem, every caviste's nightmare. Crazy cocker spaniel children, wild-eyed middle-aged Weimaraner males, riotous red setter wine students, all excitable, clumsy and out of control. As you watch in horror, praying nothing is knocked over or destroyed, your scent of fear permeating the air, just remember the same rules apply in every fine wine store for every breed around the globe.

Look 'em straight in the eye, be firm but fair and let them know who's boss.

JASON HOY HAS BEEN THE LONG-TIME MANAGER OF SYDNEY'S ULTIMO WINE CENTRE. HE HAS ALSO WRITTEN FOR *GOURMET TRAVELLER WINE* AND *MARIE CLAIRE* MAGAZINES AS WELL AS RECEIVING THE NEGOCIANTS AUSTRALIA WINE WRITING PRIZE. HE FIRMLY BELIEVES IN THE HAIR OF THE DOG.

FAVOURITE TOY: BALLS
FAVOURITE FOOD: CHEESE
OBSESSIONS: FETCHING AND SWIMMING
NAUGHTIEST DEED: RUNNING THROUGH THE GUINEA FOWL
FAVOURITE PASTIMES: MEETING AND GREETING AND BEING BRUSHED

HARRY

ASTRO

PET HATE: *BEING LEFT HOME ALONE*
FAVOURITE PASTIME: *BODYSURFING*
FAVOURITE TOY: *REINDEER HAND PUPPET*
FAVOURITE FOODS: *CHOPS AND CHICKEN NECKS*
OBSESSION: *BEING NO MORE THAN A STEP BEHIND*
KNOWN ACCOMPLICES: *CHARLIE BROWN AND YOKO*
NAUGHTIEST DEED: *EATING EVERYTHING WHEN HE WAS A PUP*

NAUGHTIEST DEED: ROUNDING UP
VERY EXPENSIVE ALPACAS AT
NEIGHBOURING ALPACA FARM
FAVOURITE FOOD:
CHOC WEDGE ICE-CREAM
OBSESSION: ROOS
FAVOURITE TOY: HIS BED
PET HATE: NOT BEING ABLE TO SCRATCH HIMSELF ANY MORE
FAVOURITE PASTIMES: SLEEPING AND DREAMING OF THE GLORY DAYS

CHARLIE BROWN

BOB

OBSESSION: STICKS
PET HATE: BEING TOLD TO GO OUTSIDE
FAVOURITE FOOD: ITALIAN TUNA IN OLIVE OIL
FAVOURITE TOY: ANYTHING THAT SASCHA RENNIE HAS
FAVOURITE PASTIME: CHASING WAVES AT BRIDPORT BEACH
NAUGHTIEST DEED: DESTROYING A PAIR OF SALVATORE FERRAGAMO SHOES

HOUSTON

FAVOURITE TOY: TEDDY
FAVOURITE FOOD: SCHMACKOS
PET HATE: GETTING INTO TROUBLE –
"HOUSTON WE HAVE A PROBLEM"
NAUGHTIEST DEED: GOING OFF HUNTING
OBSESSION: PLAYING WITH SOFT CUBDLY TEDDIES

FAVOURITE FOOD: ROAD KILL
FAVOURITE PASTIME: EATING
KNOWN ACCOMPLICES: SHEEP DOGS
NAUGHTIEST DEED: ROLLING IN ROAD KILL
PET HATE: BEING WOKEN EARLY IN THE MORNING
OBSESSION: MORNING TEA WITH THE VINEYARD WORKERS

ELLIE

LUCY

OBSESSION: FOOD
PET HATE: LOUD NOISES
FAVOURITE TOY: CHILDREN
FAVOURITE FOOD: BREADSTICKS
NAUGHTIEST DEED: BEGGING FOR FOOD AT CELLAR DOOR
FAVOURITE PASTIME: DOING PIROUETTES FOR BREAD STICKS

ALVIN PURPLE III

OBSESSION: THE BALL
FAVOURITE TOY: THE BALL
PET HATE: NOT GOING TO WORK
FAVOURITE PASTIMES: SWIMMING,
SOCIALISING AND LONG WALKS ON THE BEACH
FAVOURITE FOOD: DAVE'S BACON AND EGGS
KNOWN ACCOMPLICES: RESIDENT TASMANIAN NATIVE HENS
NAUGHTIEST DEED: THE WEEKLY ROLL IN SOMETHING SMELLY

CAPPY

PET HATE: NOT COMING IN THE UTE
NAUGHTIEST DEED: INHALING GRASS SEEDS
OBSESSION: DETECTING CYCLISTS WITH DOGS
FAVOURITE PASTIME: CHASING BIRDS IN THE VINEYARD
KNOWN ACCOMPLICE: FRANK THE NEXT-DOOR TERRIER

FAVOURITE FOOD: VEGEMITE TOAST
NAUGHTIEST DEED: UNRAVELLING A
RUG KNITTED FOR HER BY A FRIEND
OBSESSION: GUARDING STOLEN BISCUITS
PET HATE: CAPPY OCCUPYING HER DOG BASKET
FAVOURITE PASTIME: STEALING CAPPY'S BISCUITS

PEPPERCORN

OBSESSION: GOING FOR A DRIVE
FAVOURITE PASTIME: MORNING WALK THROUGH
THE VINEYARD AND DOWN TO WILD DUCK CREEK
NAUGHTIEST DEED: WANTING TO PLAY WITH THE NEXT-
DOOR HORSE AND BEING KICKED BACK OVER THE FENCE
PET HATE: THE LAY GIRLS (ARMSTEAD ESTATE CHOOKS)
KNOWN ACCOMPLICE: ARNOLD, THE NEXT-DOOR SCHNAUZER

ROXY

SHADOW

FAVOURITE PASTIMES: SCHMOOZING AND GIVING
"PAWTOGRAPHS" TO FANS AT THE CELLAR DOOR
OBSESSION: CHASING VIBRATING TRELLIS WIRE
PET HATE: PEOPLE LEAVING THE CELLAR DOOR
WITHOUT A BOTTLE OF HIS WINE, 'SHADOW'S RUN'
FAVOURITE TOYS: TRELLIS WIRE, HOSES AND STICKS
NAUGHTIEST DEED: CHASING CATS WITH HIS FRIEND PIP
KNOWN ACCOMPLICES: HELEN AND JIM'S GRANDCHILDREN AND PIP

FAVOURITE TOY: SCRABBLE
OBSESSION: REFLECTED LIGHT
FAVOURITE FOOD: JIMMIES PIZZA
NAUGHTIEST DEED: G-STRING THEFT
FAVOURITE PASTIME: SHADOW BOXING
KNOWN ACCOMPLICES: FOO, WINSTON AND BUFFY

DANTE

POPPY KING

PET HATE: BEING BATHED
FAVOURITE FOOD: BARBEQUE CHICKEN
FAVOURITE TOY: A SOFT TOY CALLED GODFREY
FAVOURITE PASTIME: CHASING BIRDS AND JAZZ THE CAT
NAUGHTIEST DEED: BRINGING ROAD KILL INSIDE THE HOUSE
OBSESSION: BEING AS CLOSE TO YOU AS POSSIBLE AT ALL TIMES

GEORGE HONEY

OBSESSION: MEN'S UNDERPANTS
NAUGHTIEST DEED: BRINGING THE
PET BANTAM CHOOKS IN THE HOUSE
FAVOURITE FOOD: NANNY MALTO MILK BISCUITS
FAVOURITE PASTIMES: CHASING CATS AND TALKING
FAVOURITE TOYS: SOCKS AND GODFREY THE SOFT TOY

NAUGHTIEST DEED: THE G-STRING FIASCO
KNOWN ACCOMPLICES: COCO, LEO AND ELIZA
FAVOURITE PASTIMES: EATING COCO'S TOYS AND
FINDING OLD ANIMAL CARCASES TO ROLL IN
PET HATE: NICK BROWN SHOOTING RABBITS NEAR THE HOUSE
OBSESSION: LICKING LEO THE CAT (THEY SEEM UNUSUALLY CLOSE)
FAVOURITE FOOD: MEDIUM RARE EYE FILLET, STRAIGHT FROM THE TABLE

VINO

PET HATE: CATS
OBSESSION: DRIVING
FAVOURITE FOODS: HARES OR RABBITS
FAVOURITE PASTIME: LYING IN THE WAY
KNOWN ACCOMPLICES: DAISY AND ZIGGY
NAUGHTIEST DEED: LOSING HER LEG TO THE FORKLIFT

KIA

MURPHY BROWN

FAVOURITE PASTIME: EATING
FAVOURITE TOY: SQUEAKY CHICKEN
PET HATE: BEING LEFT HOME ALONE
NAUGHTIEST DEED: EATING 16 MINIATURE
CHRISTMAS PUDDINGS OFF THE KITCHEN BENCH
FAVOURITE FOOD: STOLEN CELLARHAND BREAD
OBSESSION: THE BEACH AT PORT WILLUNGA IN SUMMER

DIGGORY

PET HATE: POSSUMS
FAVOURITE FOOD: OTHER PEOPLE'S
KNOWN ACCOMPLICES: TOSS AND SAM
OBSESSIONS: HIS INDEPENDENCE AND RABBITS
FAVOURITE PASTIME: BARKING AT POSSUMS ALL NIGHT
NAUGHTIEST DEED: DRAGGING DEAD RABBITS INTO CELLAR DOOR

OBSESSIONS: WASPS AND BEES
FAVOURITE TOY: BARREL BUNGS
FAVOURITE FOOD: SOMEONE ELSE'S
PET HATES: WASPS, BEES AND CATS
NAUGHTIEST DEED: ESCAPING AND
CRUISING TOWN CAFES TO BEG FOR FOOD
FAVOURITE PASTIME: CRUISING THE CAFES IN TOWN

RACHIS

BEN

FAVOURITE TOY: THONGS
PET HATE: BEING TIED UP
KNOWN ACCOMPLICES: THE GOATS
FAVOURITE PASTIME: CHASING DUCKS
NAUGHTIEST DEED: CHASING DUCKLINGS ON THE DAM
OBSESSION: BRINGING SOMETHING TO YOU WHEN YOU ARRIVE HOME

BARNABY-HOUND @ LARGE
by Nick Stock

BLOODY RECESSION!

News is just in that Doug's gone and cancelled the annual trip to France this year. Bastard! Tough times indeed. I'll keep a stiff upper lip, not that anyone will notice. With an underbite like mine there's not much to see in terms of the old top lip. For once I'm as grumpy as I look right now.

Speaking of grumpy, d'Artagnan would be disgusted. I miss him, grumpy bugger that he was. But geez he was lovable. He finally succumbed to the big 'C' when we were over in France last year and I didn't get a chance to say goodbye. He was hard to get to know (well he was a shar pei after all!) but one of the greatest friends I could ever wish for. I still see his young owner, Juanessa, stepping it out round the Tan running track up at the Domain from time to time. She always stops to say hello and gives me a scratch. She walks really fast – these wrinkly little legs would never keep up with her long skinny ones. It's been a year and she still hasn't got another dog – I bet she really wants one though. He'd be a hard act to follow. I'll keep you posted.

Just got a note from Madison my ridgeback girlfriend (not like that!) over in McLaren Vale the other day. She's put some new photos up on Pawbook. Whoa! Guess who had a great summer this year? A LOT of Champagne by the looks of it. She looks great though, her coat's all shiny from the seawater and she keeps herself tidy. She eats plenty of the best grain-fed dry-aged Coorong Black Angus with mega marbling and you'd never know it. I'd be the size of a house if I ate that stuff. Bulldog metabolism must be the slowest on record.

Speaking of great steaks, it looks like the closest I'm gonna get to the annual summer trip to France will be a few extra meals at France-Soir, our local French joint on Toorak Road. Doug calls it the 'canteen'. Hey, a few extra sessions there won't be the worst thing in the world and I'm sure Doug'll open up the wine list and extract a few Grand Cru bottles with surgeon-like precision. The cellar in that place must be huge. The list is like a phone book. Doug loves his Chablis too and there's a good chance that the Raveneau's will get a spanking over winter to wash down too many oysters. Can't say I'm a big fan of the oyster, but Doug loves 'em.

Now don't get me wrong, I love Raveneau as much as the next guy but the waiters at France-Soir tap the yellow wax capsule off with their wine knives and it startles the crap outta me if I'm within fallout distance. Quite embarrassing you might think, to be dusted on yellow wax crumbs, but a badge of honour amongst the South Yarra pooches. Respect! I wear the Raveneau with pride.

One weekend, after a Friday night visit that included a bottle of '99 Raveneau Le Clos, one of my ears started to annoy the crap outta me. I scratched away at it until Doug noticed, and boy did he laugh when he discovered I had a hunk of Raveneau's yellow wax capsule stuck in my ear. Grand Cru ear wax – very funny! He still tells the story – I pretend I'm asleep. Pretty standard.

Denise will be half delighted and half dreading the fact that Doug and I are staying home this winter. Maybe we'll go up north to Noosa or someplace warm. Anyway, looks like I'll be spending most of it down on Domain Road soaking up as much winter sun as I can. I'll get a few laps in around the Tan myself too – very social.

Geez I love a stroll around the Tan but I hate that final hill up past Melbourne Girls Grammar School. I've had to develop a clever strategy to take it in stages. Like a mini Ironman event I like to think. One of the perks of being extremely wrinkly, having a massive underbite, tiny legs, a huge gut and constantly bloodshot eyes is that chicks find you irresistible. Go figure!

So, I work like hell on the first stage of the hill and as we get close to MGGS I start giving the trees a good sniff, pour on the heavy breathing and back right off on the pace. A few upwards glances at Denise and she's pulling me over into the slow lane and then all I need then is one little guest scratcher. Only one admirer is all it takes, then two, three and then, whammo, it's on like Donkey Kong. Once I had about twenty girls crowded around. Legend!

After a good tummy rub and full body scratch we're back on the track and the rest of the hill feels like nothing. It's funny how easy exercise seems when you're feeling like a million bucks. Of course, no walk around the Tan would be complete without a quick coffee stop back along Domain Road. Denise has a good old de-brief with her girlfriends and I've taken to limbering up a bit under the table and practising all the cute poses I've been working on. You see, Denise is taking art classes and she's painting like a demon. She's doing one of me for Doug to cheer him up and take his mind away from the foie gras he WON'T be eating in France this winter. He'll love it. And if they're happy, I'm happy. You get the drift.

Hey, maybe Craig and Sue will print her painting here in Wine Dogs one day. Now THAT, would be cool!

NICK STOCK IS ONE OF AUSTRALIA'S MOST PROLIFIC WINE WRITERS. AS EDITOR OF THE PENGUIN *GOOD AUSTRALIAN WINE GUIDE*, CONTRIBUTOR TO A WIDE RANGE OF MAGAZINES, NEWSPAPER COLUMNIST AND TV PRESENTER, HE SPENDS FAR TOO LITTLE TIME AT HOME TO OWN A DOG, BUT LIVES VICARIOUSLY THROUGH REGULAR ENCOUNTERS WITH WINE DOGS THE WORLD OVER.

FAVOURITE TOY: BLUE RUBBER BALL
OBSESSION: GETTING IN THE TRACTOR
PET HATES: THUNDER AND NAIL CLIPPERS
FAVOURITE PASTIME: BEING AROUND WATER
NAUGHTIEST DEED: ROLLING IN COW MANURE
KNOWN ACCOMPLICE: THE NEW HOLLAND TRACTOR

BRONSON CHARLES

FAVOURITE TOY: MUSICAL DUCK
FAVOURITE FOOD: ROAST CHICKEN
PET HATE: NOT BEING ALLOWED ON THE BED
NAUGHTIEST DEED: DESTROYING HIS BEDDING
OBSESSION: TUGGING ON LOUISE'S APRON STRINGS
FAVOURITE PASTIME: CHASING SKIMMING STONES AT THE BEACH

BOBBY

FAVOURITE TOY: BAZ
FAVOURITE FOOD: CAT BISCUITS
NAUGHTIEST DEED: PEEING ON HANDBAGS
OBSESSION: PLAYING WITH WATER FROM THE HOSE
PET HATE: NOT BEING ABLE TO RUN AS FREELY ANYMORE
FAVOURITE PASTIME: HAVING PEOPLE TELL HIM WHAT A GOOD BOY HE IS

FAVOURITE TOY: TENNIS BALLS
FAVOURITE FOOD: ROAST CHICKEN
PET HATE: BEING LEFT BEHIND BY PHILIP
OBSESSIONS: TENNIS BALLS AND RABBITS
NAUGHTIEST DEEDS: RESHAPING PHILIP'S FAVOURITE
HAT AND RUNNING OFF WITH TOILET ROLLS
FAVOURITE PASTIME: RUNNING THROUGH THE VINEYARD

LUCCA

ROCKY

FAVOURITE PASTIME: SLEEPING
FAVOURITE TOY: BULLOCK BONE
PET HATE: CATS ON THE VERANDAH
FAVOURITE FOOD: FRIDAY BBQ LUNCH
OBSESSION: MEETING CELLAR DOOR GUESTS
NAUGHTIEST DEED: LEAVING UNWANTED PRESENTS AROUND THE WINERY

TYRRELL'S WINES POKOLBIN, NSW | GOLDEN RETRIEVER, 7 | OWNER: ANDREW PENGILLY

NAUGHTIEST DEED: CATCHING A KINGFISHER IN
MID-FLIGHT AND TAKING IT TO BED WITH HER
FAVOURITE PASTIME: TRAVELLING IN THE CAR
PET HATES: VETS AND BEING BRUSHED
OBSESSION: THE LAWNMOWER
KNOWN ACCOMPLICE: JD

SALLY

ENZO

FAVOURITE FOOD: CHICKEN WINGS
FAVOURITE PASTIME: RIDING IN CARS
FAVOURITE TOY: YELLOW PLASTIC CHICKEN
NAUGHTIEST DEED: EATING BRUCE
TYRRELL'S SLEEP APNOEA MASK – TWICE
PET HATE: RABBITS LIVING IN THE GARDEN

OBSESSION: FISHING
KNOWN ACCOMPLICE: MOËT
FAVOURITE FOOD: CHOCOLATE
PET HATE: NOT GOING FISHING
FAVOURITE TOY: STUFFED ANIMAL
FAVOURITE PASTIMES: FISHING AND SWIMMING

BARNEY

OWNERS: JULIE AND SEAN BENNETT | GOLDEN RETRIEVER, 4 | **HOME HILL WINERY** RANELAGH, TAS | 235

FAVOURITE TOY: BARNEY
PET HATE: GOING IN THE CAR
FAVOURITE FOOD: EYE FILLET
NAUGHTIEST DEED: GOING TO THE DAM AFTER GROOMING
OBSESSION: OPENING THE BACK DOOR AND LETTING HIMSELF IN
FAVOURITE PASTIMES: WALKING AND WORKING IN THE VINEYARD WITH BARNEY

MOËT

| **HOME HILL WINERY** RANELAGH, TAS | GOLDEN RETRIEVER, 8 | OWNERS: ROSEMARY AND TERRY BENNETT

FAVOURITE FOOD: PIZZA
OBSESSION: OSCAR THE CAT
FAVOURITE TOY: OSCAR THE CAT
PET HATE: NOT BEING FED ON TIME
FAVOURITE PASTIMES: SWIMMING AND WALKING
NAUGHTIEST DEED: DIGGING HOLES IN THE GARDEN

ALBERT

MAKO

PET HATE: BEER
KNOWN ACCOMPLICE: RUSTY
FAVOURITE TOY: SQUEAKY DUCK
FAVOURITE PASTIME: BEING AT WORK
NAUGHTIEST DEED: STEALING A HALF
WHEEL OF ROQUEFORT BLUE OFF THE TABLE
OBSESSION: CHASING RABBITS IN THE VINEYARD

OBSESSION: THE ALPACAS
FAVOURITE FOOD: STOLEN EGGS
FAVOURITE TOY: EMPTY DOG FOOD CANS
KNOWN ACCOMPLICE: SQUIGGLE THE CAT
FAVOURITE PASTIME: TRYING TO REMEMBER WHAT SHE
DID FIVE MINUTES AGO (THE BLONDE OF THE DOG WORLD)
NAUGHTIEST DEED: EATING THE HEN THAT LAID THE GOLDEN EGG

HOLLY AKA BRITTANY

KNOWN ACCOMPLICE: E.T. THE CAT
FAVOURITE PASTIMES: CHASING PICK-UP
TRAILERS AND ROLLING IN DEAD CARCASSES
PET HATES: BEING TIED UP AND BEING WASHED
OBSESSION: CHASING AND ROUNDING UP WINERY CARS AND TRUCKS
NAUGHTIEST DEED: EATING ALL OF THE CHEESES SET OUT FOR GUESTS

TESS

BALLAST STONE ESTATE WINERY CURRENCY CREEK, SA | BORDER COLLIE, 8 | OWNER: JOHN LOXTON

FAVOURITE PASTIMES: FOLLOWING
HER NOSE AND INSPECTING HANDBAGS
FAVOURITE FOODS: CHIPS AND CHEESE
KNOWN ACCOMPLICE: MERLOT THE KITTEN
NAUGHTIEST DEED: OPENING THE FRIDGE THEN
EATING A CHOCOLATE CAKE ON THE COUCH
PET HATE: MERLOT CHASING AND PLAYING WITH HER TAIL

MADILYN

MONTY

PET HATE: THE CAT

FAVOURITE PASTIME:
CHASING DUCKS

NAUGHTIEST DEEDS: JUMPING ON CLEAN
SHEETS AND EATING MENTOS AND TISSUES

OBSESSIONS: WHIPPER SNIPPER AND LEAF BLOWER

KNOWN ACCOMPLICE: MARGARET'S GRANDSON FINN

FAVOURITE PASTIME: SLEEPING
FAVOURITE FOOD: CHICKEN NECKS
NAUGHTIEST DEED: SWIPING BILL'S
SANDWICHES FROM THE TABLE
PET HATE: WAITING FOR HIS DINNER
OBSESSION: RIDING ON THE FARM ATV

BOGART

ROSIE
KNOWN ACCOMPLICE: JESSIE
OBSESSION: WALKS ON THE BEACH
PET HATES: THUNDER AND PARROTS
NAUGHTIEST DEED: CLAWING THE DOOR
FAVOURITE PASTIME: GOING TO THE BEACH

WILSHIM
FAVOURITE TOY: THE AFL SHERRIN FOOTY
NAUGHTIEST DEED: CHEWING THE SHERRIN
PET HATE: SOMEONE TAKING THE SHERRIN AWAY
FAVOURITE PASTIMES: RUNNING AND PLAYING BALL
OBSESSION: CHEWING AND PLAYING WITH THE SHERRIN

THOMAS WINES POKOLBIN, NSW | CATTLE DOG X, 1, AND BORDER COLLIE, 2 | OWNERS: ANDREW AND JO THOMAS

OBSESSION: SHIM
PET HATE: HAVING A BATH
FAVOURITE TOYS: SHIM AND BOOTS
FAVOURITE PASTIME: TEASING SHIM
FAVOURITE FOOD: MUM'S HOMEMADE MEAT PIE
NAUGHTIEST DEED: STEALING BOOTS AND SHOES

ROSIE

FAVOURITE FOOD: LAMB MINCE
PET HATE: BEING LEFT BEHIND
FAVOURITE TOY: ARWIN THE CAT
NAUGHTIEST DEED: DEMOLISHING HER KENNEL
OBSESSIONS: CHASING MAGPIES AND ARWIN THE CAT
FAVOURITE PASTIME: CHASING MAGPIES OUT OF THE YARD

OBSESSION: EATING
FAVOURITE TOY: ARWIN THE CAT
PET HATE: AIRBRAKES ON TRUCKS
NAUGHTIEST DEED: STEALING STRAWBERRIES
FAVOURITE PASTIMES: MAN-TRAILING AND ANNOYING EVE

WANDIN VALLEY ESTATE LOVEDALE, NSW | BLOODHOUNDS, 2 AND 1 | OWNER: MICHELLE ASHPOLE

DAKOTA

PET HATE: THE POOL
OBSESSION: WALKING
FAVOURITE FOOD: BONE
FAVOURITE TOY: SOFT ANIMALS
NAUGHTIEST DEED: CHASING DUCKS AND CHOOKS
FAVOURITE PASTIME: ESCAPING AND CHASING ANIMALS

FAVOURITE TOY: BALLS
PET HATE: WATER FROM THE HOSE
OBSESSIONS: EATING AND WALKING
NAUGHTIEST DEED: CHEWING HIS BED
FAVOURITE PASTIME: FOLLOWING DAKOTA

DEV

HORACE

FAVOURITE TOY: FRISBEE
KNOWN ACCOMPLICE: LIZZY
PET HATE: BEING LEFT AT HOME
FAVOURITE FOOD: STEAK IN GRAVY
FAVOURITE PASTIME: BEING WITH LYN
OBSESSION: FEAR OF CURTAINS BLOWING IN THE WIND

OBSESSION: WALKS
FAVOURITE TOY: TENNIS BALL
KNOWN ACCOMPLICE: HORACE
NAUGHTIEST DEED: CHEWING TEDDY
PET HATE: NOT GETTING ENOUGH EXERCISE

LIZZY

KELLY

FAVOURITE TOY: TORCH
PET HATE: STORMY WEATHER
FAVOURITE FOOD: BEEF BONES
OBSESSION: BARKING AT LIGHTS
KNOWN ACCOMPLICES: BARRY AND MUSCAT
FAVOURITE PASTIME: SWIMMING IN THE DAM
NAUGHTIEST DEED: EATING THE FAVOURITE BANTAM CHOOK

OBSESSION: FOOD
PET HATE: STORMY WEATHER
FAVOURITE PASTIME: SLEEPING
FAVOURITE FOOD: BEEF BONES
FAVOURITE TOY: RUBBER BONES
KNOWN ACCOMPLICES: KELLY AND BARRY
NAUGHTIEST DEED: WEEING ON PRODUCTS AT THE VET

MUSCAT

PET HATE: BATHS
FAVOURITE TOY: KNOT ROPE
FAVOURITE FOOD: KANGAROO
OBSESSIONS: WALKING ON THE BEACH AND HIS BRUSH
NAUGHTIEST DEED: DESTROYING HIS STUFFED ANIMALS
FAVOURITE PASTIME: RIDING ON THE JOHN DEERE GATOR

REX

FAVOURITE TOY: KNOTTED ROPE
OBSESSION: WAITING FOR
KANGAROOS AT DAWN AND DUSK
FAVOURITE FOOD: BEDTIME TREAT
NAUGHTIEST DEED: CHEWING MATTRESS COVERS
FAVOURITE PASTIME: GOING TO THE DOGGIE BEACH

PEANUT

SALLY

FAVOURITE FOOD: KABANA
PET HATES: THUNDER AND LIGHTNING
OBSESSION: PATROLLING THE CAR PARK
FAVOURITE PASTIME: LOUNGING ON THE DECK
NAUGHTIEST DEED: COLLECTING AND DISPLAYING CARRION

SUNSET WINERY KANGAROO ISLAND SA | KELPIE X 11 | OWNER: COLIN HOPKINS

FAVOURITE FOOD: GRILLED BACON
PET HATE: GOING TO SLEEP AT NIGHT
OBSESSION: LAUNCHING HIMSELF OFF COUCHES
FAVOURITE PASTIMES: STEALING TOMATOES OFF
THE VINE AND CHEWING THE WINEMAKER'S SOCKS
NAUGHTIEST DEED: CHEWING UP BRAND NEW SOCKS
KNOWN ACCOMPLICES: MADELEINE, JESSICA AND ISABELLE

LOGAN

BEAR

KNOWN ACCOMPLICE: MAX
(THE FOOTSTOOL WITH LEGS)
FAVOURITE PASTIME: CATCHING
BALLS THROWN BY CUSTOMERS
OBSESSIONS: BALLS, STICKS AND ROOS
FAVOURITE FOODS: HAM AND PEPPERONI
PET HATE: NOT BEING ALLOWED TO GO IN THE CAR

SWINGS & ROUNDABOUTS YALLINGUP, WA | RED CLOUD KELPIE X 6 | OWNERS: THERESA AND JOHN TOWNSEND

BEWARE OF THE DOG

by Peter Forrestal

IT WAS MOTHER'S DAY. The florist gasped at the dog signs, looked around, placed the flowers on the edge of the verandah, and fled – looking around for a dog who would inspire such an array of signs. He didn't catch a glimpse of the meek beagle, Fling. I suppose you can't blame couriers unfamiliar with the sense of humour that can see delight in 44 signs in about 25 languages.

It all started with 'Chien Méchant' the term I learnt at school which means 'Beware of the Dog' in French. As my wife, Elaine, and I are frequent travellers to France, it is scarcely surprising that I would notice the sign in a hardware shop one day, years ago, and think how appropriate the literal translation 'naughty dog' was to describe our beagle, Munch. That became the first sign.

Subsequent trips to France revealed, among much more, the richness of the French language and just how many subtle variations they could find for that simple English expression. We collected a few of these signs and put them up on the gate.

The late Judy Hirst invited me to join a quite remarkable media group on a food and wine trip to South Africa. While this was a seminal time for me professionally, it was also the moment when I began the hunt for the multi-lingual dog sign. I decided that the best present to bring home from the trip would be a 'Beware of the dog' sign from South Africa and so I sought an occasion to divert the group towards a hardware shop or two. What was so different about the South African signs was that they were written in English, Afrikaans and Bantu, thus giving a notion of the country's linguistic diversity.

After this, I became a collector of dog signs. Every trip had a secondary purpose. In 1997, I was with the Frescobaldi family in Milan and drove down to visit their vineyard near the ancient hilltop village of Montepulciano in Tuscany when I chanced upon a rare jewel, a sign in Latin – 'Cave Canem'. I had struggled with Latin for six years as a schoolboy and so this moment's joy was the least the language owed me.

In 1998, I was off to Greece for the International Olive Oil Conference with a lively bunch of food writers including good friends Lyndey Milan and fellow beagle fancier, Philippa

Goodrick. Because the Greek language uses the cyrillic script, this was obviously an important place for a collector such as myself. I managed to find one arresting sign with a wild dog baying at the moon and the precious cyrillic script. My pals headed off into the hills of Crete on secret women's business (probably shopping) and returned triumphantly with sign bearing a ferocious-looking Alsatian and the exotic script.

Two years later, there was a frantic drive around the ancient town of Oporto in Portugal on the last afternoon of a week's exploration of the country's cork production. We had to hunt exhaustively but, at the last minute, found the obligatory sign in Portugal's classiest hardware store. Ten days in Andalusia in Spain's south in 2002 with another group of food writers gave me many rich memories and two ornate tile signs bought on the cobbled streets of Cordoba. When Adelaide chef, Cheong Liew returned to Malaysia after 30 years he had an entourage of food and wine writers. Apart from tasting durian, loving hawker food and the like, I managed to pick up a dog sign that was different – as it was in Malaysian, English, Mandarin and Hindi.

At the end of the millennium, Elaine and I managed a house-swap with some friends from Paris and so had our first lengthy stay in the capital. One of our discoveries from a shop near Rue de Seine (and other places subsequently) were the marvellous small, stark black-and-white metal signs with a range of messages from 'Chien Lunatique' on. We bought 'Beware of the cat' on the Portabello Road in London because our Abyssinian cat, Razzy, was always much more fierce than Munch. We found a quintessentially English, solid brass sign in Oxford for £25. It seemed time for one simple expensive sign in English. At the time, we hadn't counted on Elaine's daughter, Carmel (who was living in England at the time) offering 'Never mind the dog, beware of the owner'.

As the clutter grew, it came time for a new purpose-built gate. And an avalanche of gifts. Our friends from Northern Ireland, Ian and Margaret Livingston, had one made in Gaelic; my godson, Chris Hopkins, returned from Japan with Snoopy and a Japanese message; our IT guru, Andrew Neilsen returned from a wedding in Iceland with a gift; Marshall Thompson took time off from his wet fish enterprises in Burma to buy signs for our house and his; the indomitable Wolfie returned from Italy with the shotgun cartoon; Lexie and Michael provided a Sicilian note with a reference to 'Dal Padrone'; Di Loots returned from her native South Africa with the flashest sign complete with a flag and a beagle; and perhaps best of all James and Marie-Jose Lawther linked Bordeaux and Cobb Street inextricably with 'Je habite ici... SVP fermez le portail' for us to pop Fling's photo on and add a personal touch.

We asked for the words and had some signs made to celebrate personal links: with our Welsh friend Eryl; in Polish for Barbara who has worked for us for 25 years; and in Vietnamese for Tam who has done our gardening for a similar period and so is part of the household, our extended family.

There's a poignant touch, too. Working from home you come to know the neighbourhood in ways that some might not. Elaine had accepted as a familiar sight, the letter dropper who would call past – always at 8.45am – and always call out to Munch with a chuckle 'Chien méchant'. After several years he came to the gate one day and called to us, but wouldn't come in. He had a small bundle of dog signs which he had bought in Europe, inspired by our gate. He explained that he had bone marrow cancer, had not long to live, and wanted us to have his signs. We didn't see him again but his legacy is part of the patchwork on the gate.

It's part of our story: about us and our animals; us and our friends; us and our travels; our multi-cultural, multi-lingual world. It's all said with a touch of whimsy: something to raise a smile. And remember.

BEAGLE FANCIER, **PETER FORRESTAL** WRITES WEEKLY WINE COLUMNS FOR THE *SUNDAY TIMES MAGAZINE*, THE *BULLETIN* AND THE *QUAFF* WEBSITE – WWW.QUAFF.COM.AU, AS WELL AS *QUAFF*, AN ANNUAL GUIDE TO THE BEST BUDGET-PRICED WINES IN AUSTRALIA. HE WAS FOUNDING EDITOR OF *GOURMET TRAVELLER WINE* AND HIS 30 BOOKS INCLUDE THE *GLOBAL ENCYCLOPAEDIA OF WINE*. PHOTOS BY ELAINE FORRESTAL.

PRIMITIVO (TIVO)

OBSESSION: *MICE*
PET HATE: *MICE THAT GET AWAY*
KNOWN ACCOMPLICE: *ZINFANDEL (RIP)*
NAUGHTIEST DEED: *TRYING TO HUMP A*
SMALL CHILD DURING A FORMAL WINE TASTING
FAVOURITE PASTIME: *GREETING VISITORS IN*
THEIR CAR BY RESTING HIS CHIN ON THEIR LAP

PET HATE: THUNDER
FAVOURITE FOOD: RABBIT
FAVOURITE PASTIME: ROUNDING UP THE
QUAD BIKE, HER OWNER AND THE COWS
FAVOURITE TOYS: EVERYONE AND CATTLE
OBSESSIONS: THE COUCH AND MARCUS' BED
NAUGHTIEST DEED: RIPPING SLEEVES OFF WORK SHIRTS

CHARDY

OWNER: MARCUS GILLON | KELPIE, 3 | **SNOBS CREEK ESTATE** SNOBS CREEK, VIC | 261

BARRETT

FAVOURITE FOOD: OSSO BUCCO
PET HATE: HAVING HIS FACE WASHED
FAVOURITE TOY: HECTOR THE TOY DOG
KNOWN ACCOMPLICES: LOTTI, SCUBI AND BONNY
OBSESSION: ROLLING OVER FOR TUMMY TICKLES
NAUGHTIEST DEED: NOT COMING WHEN HE'S CALLED
FAVOURITE PASTIME: LYING WITH HIS HEAD ON SOMEONE'S FOOT

OBSESSION: SOCKS
PET HATE: BATHTIME
FAVOURITE FOOD: SOCKS
KNOWN ACCOMPLICE: RUEGAR
FAVOURITE PASTIME: DIGGING HOLES
NAUGHTIEST DEED: EATING A WHOLE CHILLI PLANT

PENNY

OWNER: DARREN ATKINSON | DOBERMAN, 4 MONTHS | **BIMBADGEN ESTATE** POKOLBIN, NSW | 263

BIMBADGEN ESTATE POKOLBIN, NSW | MALTESE, 6 | OWNER: KAREN EVANS

MONTEZUMA

FAVOURITE FOOD: CHICKEN
FAVOURITE PASTIME: SNOOZING
FAVOURITE TOY: A FLUFFY HOTDOG
PET HATES: HAIRCUTS AND DOG FOOD
KNOWN ACCOMPLICES: JESSE AND NELSON
NAUGHTIEST DEED: SCRATCHING THROUGH DOORS
OBSESSIONS: CHICKEN AND FOLLOWING MUM AROUND

OBSESSION: FOOD
KNOWN ACCOMPLICES: CONFERENCE ATTENDEES
NAUGHTIEST DEED: EATING FUNDRAISER CHOCOLATES
FAVOURITE TOYS: UGG BOOTS AND INFLATED BALLOONS
FAVOURITE PASTIME: HUNTING GECKOS IN THE GARDEN
PET HATE: SMOKE ALARM BEEPS WHEN THE BATTERY RUNS LOW

SUZIE

SAMMY

PET HATE: ELECTRIC FENCES
KNOWN ACCOMPLICE: CHLOE
FAVOURITE PASTIME: CHASING RABBITS
OBSESSIONS: CHASING RABBITS AND DIGGING HOLES
NAUGHTIEST DEED: DIGGING UP LOO'S VEGIE GARDEN
FAVOURITE FOODS: BARBECUE LEFTOVERS AND RABBITS

PET HATE: BEING TIED UP
FAVOURITE FOOD: BONES
FAVOURITE TOYS: KIDS' TOYS
OBSESSION: CATCHING BUTTERFLIES
FAVOURITE PASTIME: CHASING CATTLE
NAUGHTIEST DEED: ROLLING IN COW POO

NELLY

SPOT

PET HATE: TORCHES
FAVOURITE FOOD: CRAYFISH
FAVOURITE TOY: SOCCER BALL
OBSESSIONS: BALLS AND FOOD
NAUGHTIEST DEED: EATING CARPET
FAVOURITE PASTIMES: EATING, SLEEPING AND RUNNING

FAVOURITE TOY: KONG
OBSESSIONS: UTES AND BIKES
FAVOURITE FOOD: BEEF MARROW BONES
NAUGHTIEST DEED: CHASING MOTORBIKES
PET HATES: THUNDERSTORMS AND GUNFIRE
KNOWN ACCOMPLICES: DOLLY AND TEDDY FROM NEXT DOOR
FAVOURITE PASTIME: CHASING BUTTERFLIES IN THE VINEYARD

PEPPY

FAVOURITE FOOD: LAMB
KNOWN ACCOMPLICE: RUBY
PET HATE: FIRST MEETING WITH ANYONE
OBSESSIONS: RABBITS AND HOT-AIR BALLOONS
FAVOURITE PASTIME: RIDING IN THE UTE AND TRACTOR
NAUGHTIEST DEED: BITING DAVE POWELL ON CHRISTMAS EVE

MERLOT

RASTUS

OBSESSION: KANGAROOS
PET HATES: GUNS AND WIND
FAVOURITE TOY: BALL WITH THROWING STICK
KNOWN ACCOMPLICES: SOPHIE, COCO AND FLOYD
NAUGHTIEST DEED: DESTRUCTION OF ONE OF EACH
PAIR OF THREE PAIRS OF EXPENSIVE ITALIAN SANDALS
FAVOURITE PASTIME: CHASING BIRDS AD INFINITUM

PET HATE: RABBITS
FAVOURITE FOOD: CHEESE
OBSESSION: CHASING RABBITS
KNOWN ACCOMPLICE: DERIC FROM FLYING FISH
NAUGHTIEST DEED: JUMPING OUT OF A CAR WINDOW TO CHASE RABBITS

STELLA

JACKSON

KNOWN ACCOMPLICE: JAMES
PET HATES: THE DOORBELL AND
YEARLY BLOW-DRY AT THE CLEANERS
FAVOURITE TOYS: HOSES AND SPRINKLERS
NAUGHTIEST DEED: DESTROYING AN ENTIRE
YARD, GARDEN AND SPRINKLER SYSTEM
OBSESSIONS: HOSES AND SNIFFING FOR RABBITS

FAVOURITE FOOD: RABBIT
PET HATE: BEING LEFT BEHIND
FAVOURITE TOY: HER LAZY BOY
OBSESSION: VISITING NEIGHBOURS FOR EXTRA F...
KNOWN ACCOMPLICE: OSCAR, THE NEIGHBOUR'S COOLIE
NAUGHTIEST DEED: NEIGHBOUR'S LAMBS DISAPPEARANCE
FAVOURITE PASTIME: HUNTING THE ELUSIVE RABBIT POPULATION

WOOLLY

BORIS

PET HATE: WATER
FAVOURITE TOY: RUBBER BARREL BUNGS
OBSESSIONS: BARREL BUNGS AND FETCHING BALLS AND STICKS
NAUGHTIEST DEED: HAVING SELECTIVE HEARING AT THE BEACH
FAVOURITE PASTIME: CHASING AND DESTROYING RUBBER BUNGS
KNOWN ACCOMPLICES: NATASHA, THE LATE RERUN, REBOUND, CHOCO AND LUCY

| **3 OCEANS WINE CO.** COWARAMUP, WA | STAFFORDSHIRE TERRIER, 2 | OWNERS: LUKAS FINN AND CLAIRE PURSE

OBSESSION: GOLF BALLS
FAVOURITE FOODS: SALMON STEAKS AND CHOC DROPS
FAVOURITE PASTIME: CHICKEN AND POSSUM CROWD CONTROL
NAUGHTIEST DEED: CHEWING UP MATTRESSES AND PILLOWS
PET HATE: POSSUMS ON THE ROOF

CHOCCO MUTLEY

LUCY

FAVOURITE FOOD: CAROB
OBSESSION: HIDING TOYS
PET HATE: BEING LEFT OUT
FAVOURITE PASTIME: SWIMMING
NAUGHTIEST DEED: CHEWING THE CAR INTERIOR

KNOWN ACCOMPLICE: BLACKJACK THE CAT
(THOUGH NOT PUBLICLY ACKNOWLEDGED)
FAVOURITE TOY: PLASTIC SQUEAKING DUMB BELL
NAUGHTIEST DEED: LICKING THE ANKLES OF A
GERMAN BACKPACKER WHILST SHE WAS TRYING TO TASTE
FAVOURITE PASTIMES: CHASING BALLS, STICKS AND HARES
FAVOURITE FOODS: LIVER AND HEARTS COOKED WITH RICE

HENRY RUSSELL

NAUGHTIEST DEED: DIGGING UP AND REBURYING MUDDY BONES UNDER LARA'S BED
FAVOURITE PASTIME: CHASING THE QUADDIE OR THE WINERY BOBTAIL
FAVOURITE FOOD: ROAST LAMB WITH HOMEMADE GRAVY
PET HATE: NOT BEING ALLOWED TO RIDE UP FRONT
OBSESSIONS: CAFFEINE AND THE COFFEE GRINDER
KNOWN ACCOMPLICES: ZOË AND LACEY
FAVOURITE TOY: ANY STICK OR TWIG

OBAN

ALDERSYDE ESTATE BICKLEY, WA | BORDER COLLIE, 5 | OWNER: LARA BRAY

OBSESSION: OBAN
FAVOURITE FOOD: FREE-RANGE CHICKEN
PET HATE: THE CUTLERY DRAWER BEING OPENED
FAVOURITE TOYS: FEATHER PILLOWS OR CUSHIONS
NAUGHTIEST DEED: STEALING THE AFTERNOON TEA CAKE
FAVOURITE PASTIME: MORNING RUNS THROUGH THE ORCHARD

ZOË

MOLLY

PET HATE: FAST RABBITS
OBSESSION: POSSUMS IN THE SHED
NAUGHTIEST DEED: ROLLING IN MUD
FAVOURITE PASTIME: CHASING KANGAROOS
KNOWN ACCOMPLICE: HARRY THE GOLDEN RETRIEVER

PET HATE: SHOTGUNS
KNOWN ACCOMPLICE: CHOPPER THE CAT
FAVOURITE PASTIME: PLAYING WITH KIDS
NAUGHTIEST DEED: CHEWING THE WIFE'S
ONLY PAIR OF SHOES THAT WENT TO AFRICA
FAVOURITE TOY: CHOPPER, THE REAL LIFE CAT
OBSESSIONS: CHEWING SHOES AND BIKE SEATS

MOLLY

JEDDA

PET HATE: *WASHING*
FAVOURITE TOY: *TENNIS BALL*
KNOWN ACCOMPLICE: *BRIAN*
NAUGHTIEST DEED: *SCOFFING THE CAT'S TUCKER*
FAVOURITE PASTIME: *FETCHING BALLS IN THE SURF*
OBSESSIONS: *BEING CLOSE BY AND THINGS THAT MOVE*

OBSESSION: CATS
PET HATE: GUNSHOTS
KNOWN ACCOMPLICE: ERNIE
FAVOURITE FOOD: KANGAROO
NAUGHTIEST DEED: MAULING A CHICKEN
FAVOURITE PASTIME: SLEEPING IN HIS OWNER'S UTE

MAX

DERIC

FAVOURITE FOOD: HIS LAMB BONES
OBSESSIONS: BALLS, STICKS AND KIDS
NAUGHTIEST DEED: URINATING ON BALLS
 AND GETTING PEOPLE TO PICK THEM UP
KNOWN ACCOMPLICES: BEAR AND SLY DOG BENDER
PET HATE: GETTING LESS ATTENTION THAN MINKY THE CAT
FAVOURITE PASTIMES: BEACH, BALLS, STICKS AND KIDS

FAVOURITE FOOD: CHEESE
FAVOURITE TOY: SQUEAKY TOYS
OBSESSION: CHASING TORCH LIGHT
PET HATES: SKATEBOARDS AND SCOOTERS
FAVOURITE PASTIME: RIDING IN THE FRONT SEAT OF THE CAR
NAUGHTIEST DEED: STEALING BREAD FROM THE PET BULL AND CHICKENS

SHIRAZ

FAVOURITE FOOD: BONES
PET HATE: WORMING PILLS
FAVOURITE TOY: STUFFED RABBIT
KNOWN ACCOMPLICES: KIM AND NESS
OBSESSION: CHASING DUCKS OFF THE DAM
FAVOURITE PASTIME: SWIMMING AT THE BEACH AND DAM

GUS

PET HATE: FOXES
OBSESSION: FOXES
FAVOURITE FOOD: COLES BARBEQUE CHOOK
FAVOURITE PASTIME: PATROLLING FOR FOXES
NAUGHTIEST DEED: EATING A FULL TUB OF BUTTER THAT WASN'T HIS

BARNEY

OSCAR

PET HATE: COURIERS
OBSESSION: GUARDING
FAVOURITE PASTIME: SLEEPING
NAUGHTIEST DEED: SCARING COURIERS
FAVOURITE TOYS: THE BOYS, FLYNN AND TEAGUE

PET HATE: *SMOKEY THE CAT*
FAVOURITE PASTIME: *BEING THE MEET-
AND-GREET HOSTESS AT CELLAR DOOR*
OBSESSION: *RIDING ON THE QUAD BIKE*
KNOWN ACCOMPLICES: *OSCAR AND ZIGGY*
FAVOURITE FOOD: *GOURMET TREATS FROM BUS DRIVERS*
NAUGHTIEST DEED: *SCRATCHING AT THE CELLAR DOOR TO GET IN*

MOLLY

GEORGIA

FAVOURITE FOOD: JAM ON TOAST
FAVOURITE TOY: BALL ON A ROPE
FAVOURITE PASTIMES: CHASING BUTTERFLIES
AND DRIVING AROUND WITH CLINT
PET HATES: VACUUM CLEANERS AND BROOMS
OBSESSION: BREAKING INTO THE HOUSE TO STEAL LAUNDRY
NAUGHTIEST DEED: STEALING BUNGS FROM THE WINERY

SILKWOOD WINES PEMBERTON, WA | KELPIE X, 1 | OWNER: CLINT DECAMPO

KNOWN ACCOMPLICE: JESSIE
PET HATES: FOXES AND RABBITS
FAVOURITE FOODS: DICED STEAK AND COOKED RICE
OBSESSIONS: TENNIS BALLS AND REGULAR MORNING WALKS
FAVOURITE PASTIME: CHASING TENNIS BALLS – TWO AT A TIME
NAUGHTIEST DEED: CHEWING UP ROGER'S FAVOURITE OLD WORK HAT,
ENDING UP WITH THE RIM AROUND HIS NECK

TOBY

PET HATE: BATHS
KNOWN ACCOMPLICE: HIS BROTHER WINSTON
OBSESSION: STEALING FOOD FROM BABY ELLIS
NAUGHTIEST DEED: CHEWING THROUGH THE UTE'S FUEL LINE
FAVOURITE PASTIMES: CHASING KANGAROOS AND LYING IN THE SUN

PET HATE: INTRUDERS
FAVOURITE TOY: TOY RACCOON
OBSESSIONS: FOOD AND PLAYING
FAVOURITE PASTIMES: HANGING OUT
WITH TANIA AND CHASING SPIKE THE CAT
KNOWN ACCOMPLICES: MAKKA AND SPIKE THE CAT
NAUGHTIEST DEED: CHASING THE NEIGHBOUR'S SHEEP

KAOS

YOGI BEAR

FAVOURITE PASTIMES: SLEEPING AND
STROLLING THROUGH THE VINEYARD
OBSESSION: BIRDS FLYING IN THE SKY
FAVOURITE FOODS: TUNA AND LAMB SHANKS
NAUGHTIEST DEED: DESTROYING THE GARDEN
FAVOURITE TOYS: SQUEAKY TOYS AND TENNIS BALLS

ARE WE BARKING MAD?
by Craig McGill

WINE DOGS WAS BORN from a wine-tasting expedition through McLaren Vale and the Barossa Valley back in the late 1990s. Sue and I were greeted by pooches in almost every winery we visited; they would roll over for a tummy rub when we arrived and pose for a photo before escorting us in for a taste of the proprietor's wine. Looking back at the collection of dogs we'd met on that first trip, I flippantly suggested to Sue "there is probably a book in this!" There was no science to this idea at all – just a simple observation that wherever wine is made, you're likely to find a dog scouting the cellar door or winery.

A friend of ours, Jim Kelly, once told us that most people only have one good idea in a lifetime – and he thought Wine Dogs was ours. Now this was high praise indeed, as Jim is a highly-respected scientist whose team modified the molecular structure of collagen to increase its benefits and applications. I sat there silently listening to Jim sing our praise while thinking, "Why the hell wasn't our one good idea to do with collagen?" Sue and I knew Wine Dogs was a great idea but let's face it, we knew next-to-nothing about publishing and didn't know where to start in regards in selling or distributing a book. While every second person is sticking their head in a tub of collagen in a daily anti-ageing skincare ritual, the chances of us getting everyone to buy a copy of our book looked remote. But it wasn't long before we knew we had tapped into a much-loved theme that translated across wineries worldwide; every winery has a dog, as much a part of the winery as the cellar hand and as much loved as any family member.

Not everyone saw our idea as a stroke of genius. I recall one winemaker politely emailing us that Wine Dogs was one of the most stupid ideas he'd ever heard of and he'd be quite surprised if we ever sold a single copy. We knew Wine Dogs was an original and quirky idea but maybe this winemaker was right and we wouldn't sell a single copy. Our initial call-for-entries was even heralded at a wine industry conference "as an example of what is wrong with the wine industry." After all, wine is a serious business and these clowns aren't going to make light of our industry or our dogs!

To say that Sue and I were initially nervous about our investment would be a gross understatement. Luckily, most winemakers immediately grasped the concept and recognised how important their dogs were to the ambience of the winery. I remember having a beer with Peter Lehmann where he kindly did a ring-around to local Barossa winemakers telling them I was in the area photographing for Wine Dogs and was gob-smacked when a fellow winemaker didn't have a dog. "You can't make good wine without a dog!" he bemoaned to his colleague. Peter Lehmann has always had a long succession of dogs and has been an enthusiastic supporter of our book since its conception. "You're onto a winner there," he'd say to me. It was industry greats like Peter that re-affirmed our confidence to keep going.

Wine Dogs has since been proven to be a unique and popular book that promotes the Australian wine industry – indicated by the number of overseas wine industry people that want us to document their country's hounds. But there certainly wasn't any grand plan for a global publishing empire built around the Wine Dogs brand – we only had the modest expectation of publishing a beautiful book and perhaps making our money back in a few years. Eight editions later and we often think of that first negative email that arrived and wonder whether we should send that winemaker a copy – naaah, he can buy his own!

As simple as this idea was, it has grown into an incredible adventure for us that has taken us around the world several times, visiting thousands of the most famous wineries on the planet. It's been a fun ride so far, with no signs of slowing up – and no, you can't have our jobs! But deep down, we're still looking for that second great idea...

ALL PHOTOGRAPHY © CRAIG McGILL 2009

SUSAN ELLIOTT

**AUTHOR / PUBLISHER /
DESIGNER** *SYDNEY, NSW*

Stella and Sue

SUSAN IS A MULTI-SKILLED ARTIST WITH A BACKGROUND IN FINE ART, ILLUSTRATION AND PRINTMAKING. AFTER COMPLETING TWO YEARS OF A PSYCHOLOGY DEGREE, SUE CHANGED TO A CAREER IN ART. SHE GRADUATED FROM THE CITY ART INSTITUTE IN 1986, MAJORING IN DRAWING, PRINTMAKING AND PAINTING.

AFTER TWO YEARS LIVING ABROAD, SUE RETURNED TO AUSTRALIA AND EXHIBITED HER GRAPHIC ART AND SCREENPRINTS EXTENSIVELY AROUND SYDNEY, WHILE ALSO WORKING IN A NUMBER OF SMALL DESIGN STUDIOS. SHE HAS DEVELOPED INTO AN AWARD-WINNING GRAPHIC DESIGNER WITH OVER 20 YEARS OF EXPERIENCE IN THE INDUSTRY.

SUE JOINED McGILL DESIGN GROUP IN 1999 AS CO-OWNER AND CREATIVE DIRECTOR. SHE IS ALSO CO-FOUNDER AND PRINCIPAL OF THE GIANT DOG PUBLISHING HOUSE, WHICH IS RESPONSIBLE FOR PRODUCING A NUMBER OF BEST-SELLING BOOKS, INCLUDING THE WINE DOGS AND FOOTY DOGS TITLES.

FAVOURITE FOOD: NOODLES
OBSESSIONS: BATH SALTS AND CRYPTIC CROSSWORDS
FAVOURITE PASTIME: WATCHING MOVIES WITH STELLA
NAUGHTIEST DEED: BAD LATIN DANCING
KNOWN ACCOMPLICE: GHOST KNIFE FISH
PET HATES: WHISTLING AND PEEL IN RAISIN TOAST

SUE'S KNOWLEDGE OF DOGS IS UNPARALLELED, AND IN THE PAST SHE HAS ALSO FOUND TIME TO BE A SUCCESSFUL SIBERIAN HUSKY BREEDER. SHE IS CONSIDERED AMONGST THE PACK TO BE A GREAT OWNER. SUE IS A LOVER OF ALL WHITE WINE AND USUALLY REACHES FOR HER FAVOURITE RIESLING WHEN FEELING A LITTLE HUSKY.

GIANT DOG PUBLISHING

GIANT DOG IS A NICHE INDEPENDENT PUBLISHING HOUSE SPECIALISING IN PRODUCING BENCHMARK QUALITY DESIGN AND ART BOOKS. RECENT PUBLICATIONS INCLUDE *WINE DOGS ITALY*, *WINE DOGS AUSTRALIA*, *WINE DOGS NEW ZEALAND*, *WINE DOGS DELUXE EDITION*, *FOOTY DOGS*, *WINE DOGS: USA EDITION* AND *WINE DOGS USA 2*. www.giantdog.com.au

CRAIG McGILL

AUTHOR / PUBLISHER / PHOTOGRAPHER *SYDNEY, NSW*

ORIGINALLY FROM SHEPPARTON, VICTORIA, CRAIG IS A SELF-TAUGHT DESIGNER AND ILLUSTRATOR WHO STARTED HIS OWN DESIGN BUSINESS IN MELBOURNE AT 18 YEARS OF AGE. DURING THAT TIME HE WAS APPOINTED AS A DESIGN CONSULTANT TO THE RESERVE BANK OF AUSTRALIA.

HIS DESIGNS AND ILLUSTRATIONS HAVE GRACED BANKNOTES THROUGHOUT THE WORLD, INCLUDING THE AUSTRALIAN BICENTENARY TEN-DOLLAR NOTE. HIS WORK APPEARS ON THE ORIGINAL AUSTRALIAN $100 NOTE, PAPUA NEW GUINEA KINA, COOK ISLAND DOLLARS AND ENGLISH POUND TRAVELLER'S CHEQUES. CRAIG WAS ALSO INVOLVED IN THE DESIGN AND ILLUSTRATION OF MANY COUNTRIES' SECURITY DOCUMENTS SUCH AS PASSPORTS, BONDS AND TRAVELLER'S CHEQUES.

AT THE AGE OF 23 HE DESIGNED THE ENTIRE SERIES OF THE COOK ISLAND BANKNOTES AND IT IS BELIEVED THAT HE WAS THE WORLD'S YOUNGEST DESIGNER TO DESIGN A COUNTRY'S COMPLETE CURRENCY. IN 1991, CRAIG MOVED TO SYDNEY WHERE HIS ILLUSTRATIONS WERE REGULARLY COMMISSIONED BY AGENCIES AND DESIGNERS BOTH IN AUSTRALIA AND AROUND THE WORLD.

Craig and Tarka

PHOTOGRAPH © SUSAN ELLIOTT 2008

DATE OF BIRTH: DEAD IN DOG YEARS
FAVOURITE FOOD: ROAST DUCK AND PINOT NOIR
FAVOURITE PASTIMES: VENTRILOQUISM AND BEING A BIG KID
NAUGHTIEST DEED: CHASING HUSKIES WHILE STARK NAKED
OBSESSIONS: BEER, WINE AND COLLECTING USELESS THINGS
KNOWN ACCOMPLICES: THE VOICES IN MY HEAD
PET HATE: UNORIGINAL IDEAS

HE IS NOW WIDELY KNOWN AS AUSTRALIA'S ONLY FREELANCE CURRENCY DESIGNER. CRAIG HAS ALSO DESIGNED AND ILLUSTRATED FIVE STAMPS FOR AUSTRALIA POST.

CRAIG HAS BEEN CREATIVE DIRECTOR OF HIS OWN AGENCY, McGILL DESIGN GROUP, FOR OVER TWENTY-FIVE YEARS.

HAVING GROWN UP WITH A SUCCESSION OF BEAGLES, CRAIG IS NOW OWNED BY TWO SIBERIAN HUSKIES. www.realnasty.com.au

McGILL DESIGN GROUP

McGILL DESIGN GROUP WAS FORMED IN 1981 AND SPECIALISES IN PROVIDING A WIDE RANGE OF QUALITY GRAPHIC DESIGN SERVICES. THE STUDIO HAS PRODUCED NUMEROUS FINE WINE LABELS AND PACKAGING AS WELL AS CORPORATE IDENTITIES, ADVERTISING, PUBLICATIONS AND TELEVISION COMMERCIALS. www.mcgilldesigngroup.com

WINERY AND VINEYARD LISTINGS

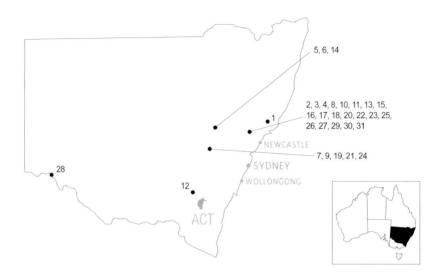

5, 6, 14

2, 3, 4, 8, 10, 11, 13, 15,
16, 17, 18, 20, 22, 23, 25,
26, 27, 29, 30, 31

1

NEWCASTLE

7, 9, 19, 21, 24

SYDNEY

28

WOLLONGONG

12

ACT

NEW SOUTH WALES

1. Alderley Creek Vineyard PAGE 163
2653 The Bucketts Way, Stroud NSW 2425
Ph: (02) 4994 5556
www.alderleycreekwines.com.au

2. Arrowfield Estate Wines PAGE 129
3483 Golden Hwy, Jerry's Plains NSW 2330
Ph: (02) 6576 4041
www.arrowfieldestate.com.au

3. Ballabourneen Wine Co. PAGE 90
2347 Broke Rd, Pokolbin NSW 2320
Ph: (02) 4998 6505
www.ballabourneen.com.au

4. Bimbadgen Estate PAGES 262–264
790 McDonalds Rd, Pokolbin NSW 2320
Ph: (02) 4998 4600
www.bimbadgen.com.au

5. Burnbrae Winery and Vineyard PAGE 106
548 Hill End Rd, Mudgee NSW 2850
Ph: (02) 6373 3504
www.burnbraewines.com.au

6. Burrundulla Vineyards PAGES 52, 53
234 Castlereagh Hwy, Mudgee NSW 2850
Ph: (02) 6372 9532
www.burrundulla.com.au

7. Cargo Road Winery PAGE 260
Cargo Rd, Orange NSW 2800
Ph: (02) 6365 6100
www.cargoroadwines.com.au

8. Catherine Vale PAGE 102
656 Milbrodale Rd, Bulga NSW 2330
Ph: (02) 6579 1334
www.catherinevale.com.au

9. Cumulus Wines PAGE 202
Davys Plains Rd, Cudal NSW 2864
Ph: (02) 6390 7900
www.cumuluswines.com.au

10. De Bortoli Wines, Hunter Valley
PAGE 228
532 Wine Country Drive, Pokolbin NSW 2320
Ph: (02) 4993 8800
www.debortoli.com.au

11. Draytons Family Wines PAGE 167
555 Oakey Creek Rd, Pokolbin NSW 2321
Ph: (02) 4998 7513
www.draytonswines.com.au

12. Gundagai Wines Australia PAGE 29
Nargoon Cellar Door, 554 Nangus Rd,
*   Gundagai NSW 2722*
Ph: (02) 6944 2038
www.gundagaiwines.com.au

13. Hungerford Hill Wines PAGE 15
1 Broke Rd, Pokolbin NSW 2320
Ph: (02) 4990 0713
www.hungerfordhill.com.au

14. Huntington Estate PAGE 95
Cassillis Rd, Mudgee NSW 2850
Ph: (02) 6373 3825
www.huntingtonestate.com.au

15. Kevin Sobels Wines PAGE 161
5 Halls Rd, Pokolbin NSW 2320
Ph: (02) 4998 7766
www.sobelswines.com.au

16. Krinklewood Biodynamic
*   Vineyard* PAGES 88, 89
712 Wollombi Rd, Broke NSW 2330
Ph: (02) 6579 1322
www.krinklewood.com

17. Mabrook Estate PAGE 116
258 Inlet Rd, Bulga NSW 2330
Ph: (02) 9971 9994
www.mabrookestate.com

18. Margan Family Winegrowers PAGE 27
1238 Milbrodale Rd, Broke NSW 2330
Ph: (02) 6579 1317
www.margan.com.au

19. Mayfield Vineyard PAGES 16, 17
954 Icely Rd, Orange NSW 2800
Ph: (02) 6365 9293
www.mayfieldvineyard.com

20. Molly Morgan Vineyard PAGE 294
496 Talga Rd, Lovedale NSW 2320
Ph: (02) 4930 7695
www.mollymorgan.com

21. Mortimers Wines PAGES 84, 85
780 Burrendong Way, Orange NSW 2800
Ph: (02) 6365 8689
www.mortimerswines.com.au

22. Oakvale PAGES 120, 121
1596 Broke Rd, Pokolbin NSW 2320
Ph: (02) 4998 7088
www.oakvalewines.com.au

23. Pepper Tree Wines PAGE 125
Halls Rd, Pokolbin NSW 2320
Ph: (02) 4998 7539
www.peppertreewines.com.au

24. Philip Shaw Wines PAGE 231
Koomooloo Vineyard,
45 Caldwell Lane, Borenore NSW 2800
Ph: (02) 6365 2334
www.philipshaw.com.au

25. Tamburlaine Wines PAGE 164
358 McDonalds Rd, Pokolbin NSW 2321
Ph: (02) 4998 7570
www.mywinery.com

26. Tempus Two PAGE 37
Cnr Broke and McDonalds Rds,
*   Pokolbin NSW 2320*
Ph: (02) 4993 3999
www.tempustwowinery.com.au

27. Thomas Wines PAGES 244, 245
Hermitage Rd, Pokolbin NSW 2320
Ph: (02) 6574 7371
www.thomaswines.com.au

28. Trentham Estate PAGE 155
Sturt Hwy, Trentham Cliffs NSW 2738
Ph: (03) 5024 8888
www.trenthamestate.com.au

29. Tyrrell's Wines PAGES 232–234
Broke Rd, Pokolbin NSW 2320
Ph: (02) 4993 7000
www.tyrrells.com.au

30. Wandin Valley Estate PAGE 246
Wilderness Rd, Lovedale NSW 2320
Ph: (02) 4930 7317
www.wandinvalley.com.au

31. Wirral Grange Vineyard PAGE 93
168 Lomas Lane, Lovedale NSW 2325
Ph: (02) 4991 2874
www.wirralgrange.com.au

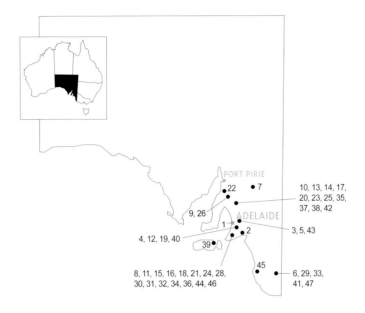

SOUTH AUSTRALIA

**1. Australian Wine and Brandy
 Corporation** PAGE 265
*Industry House, National Wine Centre,
 Cnr Hackney and Botanic Rds,
 Adelaide SA 5000*
Ph: (08) 8228 2000
www.wineaustralia.com/australia

2. Ballast Stone Estate Winery PAGE 240
*Lot 8, Myrtle Grove Rd,
 Currency Creek SA 5214*
Ph: (08) 8555 4215
www.ballaststonewines.com

3. Barratt Wines PAGES 50, 51
Cornish Rd, Summertown SA 5141
Ph: (08) 8390 1788
www.barrattwines.com.au

4. Bendbrook PAGE 192
Section 19, Pound Rd, Macclesfield SA 5153
Ph: (08) 8388 9773
www.bendbrookwines.com.au

5. BK Wines PAGE 94
Sydney Rd, Nairne SA 5252
Ph: (08) 8389 6984
www.bkwines.com.au

6. Blok Estate Coonawarra PAGE 274
Lot 1, Riddoch Hwy, Coonawarra SA 5263
Ph: (08) 8737 2734
www.blok.com.au

7. Burk Salter Wines PAGE 19
Lot 4, Paisley Rd, Blanchetown SA 5357
Ph: (08) 8540 5023
www.burksalterwines.com.au

8. Chapel Hill PAGE 86
1 Chapel Hill Rd, McLaren Vale SA 5171
Ph: (08) 8323 8429
www.chapelhillwine.com.au

9. Crabtree Wines PAGE 182
1 North Terrace, Watervale SA 5452
Ph: (08) 8843 0069
www.crabtreewines.com.au

10. Creed of Barossa PAGES 148, 149
PO Box 481, Lyndoch SA 5351
Ph: (08) 8524 4046
www.creedwines.com

11. Dandelion Vineyards PAGE 138
PO Box 138 McLaren Vale SA 5171
Ph: (08) 8556 6099
www.dandelionvineyards.com.au

12. Deviation Road PAGE 217
RMB 214, Scott Creek Rd,
 Longwood SA 5153
Ph: (08) 8339 2633
www.deviationroad.com

13. Epsilon Wines PAGE 283
Moppa Springs Rd, Greenock SA 5360
Ph: (08) 8562 8494
www.epsilonwines.com.au

14. Flaxman Wines PAGE 87
Flaxmans Valley Rd, Angaston SA 5353
Ph: (08) 8565 3288
www.flaxmanwines.com.au

15. Foggo Wines PAGE 193
Lot 21, Foggos Rd, McLaren Vale SA 5171
Ph: (08) 8323 0131
www.foggowines.com.au

16. Fox Creek Wines PAGE 216
Malpas Rd, Willunga SA 5172
Ph: (08) 8556 2403
www.foxcreekwines.com

17. Gibson Wines PAGE 271
Willows Rd, Light Pass SA 5355
Ph: (08) 8562 4224
www.gibsonwines.com.au

18. Griffin Wines PAGE 170
Tynan Rd, Kuitpo SA 5172
Ph: 0408 808 123
www.griffinwines.com

19. Hahndorf Hill Winery PAGES 112, 113
Pains Rd, Hahndorf SA 5245
Ph: (08) 8388 7512
www.hahndorfhillwinery.com.au

20. Hentley Farm PAGES 198, 199
Cnr Jenke and Gerald Roberts Rds,
 Seppeltsfield SA 5352
Ph: (08) 8562 8427
www.hentleyfarm.com.au

21. Hugh Hamilton PAGE 151
McMurtrie Rd, McLaren Vale SA 5171
Ph: (08) 8323 8689
www.hughhamiltonwines.com.au

22. Hummocks Station PAGE 270
Barunga Homestead Rd, Snowtown SA 5520
Accommodation and Functions
Ph: 0417 084 377
www.hummocks-station.com.au

23. Kalleske PAGE 185
6 Murray St, Greenock SA 5360
Ph: (08) 8563 4000
www.kalleske.com

24. Kay Brothers Amery Winery PAGE 101
Kays Rd, McLaren Vale SA 5171
Ph: (08) 8323 8201
www.kaybrothersamerywines.com

25. Kies Family Wines PAGE 194
Barossa Valley Hwy, Lyndoch SA 5351
Ph: (08) 8524 4110
www.kieswines.com.au

26. Kirrihill Wines PAGE 166
Farrell Flat Rd, Clare SA 5453
Ph: (08) 8842 1233
www.kirrihillwines.com.au

**27. Knappstein Enterprise Winery
 and Brewery** PAGE 197
2 Pioneer Ave, Clare SA 5453
Ph: (08) 8841 2100
www.knappstein.com.au

28. Lady Bay Vineyard PAGE 282
Willis Drive, Normanville SA 5024
Ph: (08) 8445 1533
www.ladybay.com.au

29. Leconfield Winery PAGES 266–268
Riddoch Hwy, Coonawarra SA 5263
Ph: (08) 8737 2326
www.leconfieldwines.com.au

**30. McLaren Vale Vine Improvement
 Society** PAGE 295
Little Rd, Willunga SA 5172
Ph: (08) 8552 6152

31. Noon Winery PAGE 180
Rifle Range Rd, McLaren Vale SA 5171
Ph: (08) 8323 8290
www.noonwinery.com.au

32. Oliver's Taranga PAGES 130, 131
Seaview Rd, McLaren Vale SA 5171
Ph: (08) 8323 8498
www.oliverstaranga.com

33. Patrick T Wines PAGE 275
Riddoch Hwy, Coonawarra SA 5263
Ph: (08) 8737 3687
www.patricktwines.com

34. Paxton PAGES 146, 147
Lot 100, Wheaton Rd, McLaren Vale SA 5171
Ph: (08) 8323 9131
www.paxtonvineyards.com

35. Peter Seppelt Wines PAGES 168, 169
Dewells Rd, Mt Pleasant SA 5235
Ph: (08) 8568 2452
www.peterseppeltwines.com.au

36. Rymill Coonawarra PAGE 12
Riddoch Hwy, Coonawarra SA 5263
Ph: (08) 8736 5001
www.rymill.com.au

37. Seppeltsfield Wines PAGES 152, 153
Seppeltsfield Rd, Seppeltsfield SA 5355
Ph: (08) 8568 6200
www.seppeltsfield.com.au

38. Smallfry Wines PAGE 279
13 Murray St, Angaston SA 5353
Ph: (08) 8564 2182
www.smallfrywines.com.au

39. Sunset Winery Kangaroo Island
PAGE 254
Hog Bay Rd, Penneshaw SA 5222
Ph: (08) 8553 1378
www.sunset-wines.com.au

40. The Lane Vineyard PAGES 136, 137
Ravenswood Lane, Hahndorf SA 5245
Ph: (08) 8388 1250
www.thelane.com.au

41. The Poplars Coonawarra PAGE 195
Riddoch Hwy, Coonawarra SA 5263
Ph: (08) 8736 3130
www.thepoplarswinery.com

42. Torbreck Vintners PAGE 38
Roennfeldt Rd, Marananga SA 5355
Ph: (08) 8562 4155
www.torbreck.com

43. Totino Estate PAGE 188
100 Murray Rd, Paracombe SA 5132
Ph: (08) 8349 1200
www.totinowines.com.au

44. Vincognita Wines PAGE 255
Nangkita Rd, Nangkita SA 5210
Ph: (08) 8370 5737
www.vincognita.com.au

45. Wehl's Mount Benson Vineyards
PAGE 145
Wrights Bay Rd, Mount Benson SA 5275
Ph: (08) 8768 6251
www.wehlsmtbensonvineyards.com.au

46. Wirra Wirra Vineyards PAGE 221
McMurtrie Rd, McLaren Vale SA 5171
Ph: (08) 8323 8414
www.wirrawirra.com

47. Zema Estate PAGES 186, 187
Riddoch Hwy, Coonawarra SA 5263
Ph: (08) 8736 3219
www.zema.com.au

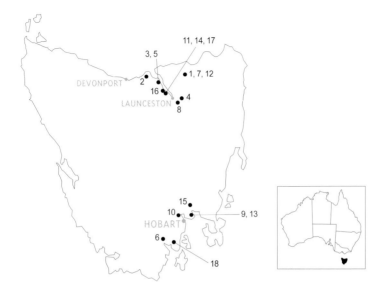

TASMANIA

1. Brook Eden PAGE 115
167 Adams Rd, Lebrina TAS 7254
Ph: (03) 6395 6244
www.brookeden.com.au

2. Ghost Rock Vineyard PAGE 162
1055 Port Sorell Rd, Northdown TAS 7307
Ph: (03) 6428 4005
www.ghostrock.com.au

3. Goaty Hill Wines PAGE 230
Auburn Rd, Kayena TAS 7270
Ph: (03) 6391 9090
www.goatyhill.com

4. Gryphonwood Vineyards PAGES 56, 57
218 Underwood Rd, Underwood TAS 7268
Ph: (03) 6395 1061

5. Holm Oak Vineyards PAGES 122–124
11 West Bay Rd, Rowella TAS 7270
Ph: (03) 6394 7577
www.holmoakvineyards.com.au

6. Home Hill Winery PAGES 235–237
38 Nairn St, Ranelagh TAS 7109
Ph: (03) 6264 1200
www.homehillwines.com.au

7. Jansz Tasmania PAGE 210
1216B Pipers Brook Rd,
*   Pipers Brook TAS 7254*
Ph: (03) 6382 7066
www.jansztas.com

8. Josef Chromy PAGE 213
370 Relbia Rd, Relbia TAS 7258
Ph: (03) 6335 8700
www.josefchromy.com.au

9. Meadowbank Wines PAGE 211
699 Richmond Rd, Cambridge TAS 7170
Ph: (03) 6248 4484
www.meadowbankwines.com.au

10. Moorilla PAGES 21–23
655 Main Rd, Berriedale TAS 7011
Ph: (03) 6277 9900
www.moorilla.com.au

11. Ninth Island Vineyard PAGES 247, 248
95 Rosevears Drive, Rosevears TAS 7277
Ph: (03) 6330 2388
www.kreglingerwineestates.com

12. Pipers Brook Vineyard PAGE 103
1216 Pipers Brook Rd,
* Pipers Brook TAS 7254*
Ph: (03) 6382 7527
www.kreglingerwineestates.com

13. Puddleduck Vineyard PAGES 40, 41
992 Richmond Rd, Richmond TAS 7025
Ph: (03) 6260 2301
www.puddleduckvineyard.com.au

14. Rosevears Vineyard PAGE 196
1A Waldhorn Drive, Rosevears TAS 7277
Ph: (03) 6330 1800
www.rosevears.com.au

15. Roslyn Estate PAGE 269
409 White Kangaroo Rd, Campania TAS 7026
Ph: (03) 6260 4077
www.roslynestate.com.au

16. Stoney Rise Wine Company PAGE 18
96 Hendersons Lane,
* Gravelly Beach TAS 7276*
Ph: (03) 6394 3678
www.stoneyrise.com

17. Strathlynn Winery PAGE 249
95 Rosevears Drive, Rosevears TAS 7277
Ph: (03) 6330 2388

18. Two Bud Spur PAGE 128
By appointment only
1033 Woodbridge Hill Rd,
* Gardners Bay TAS 7112*
www.twobudspur.com.au

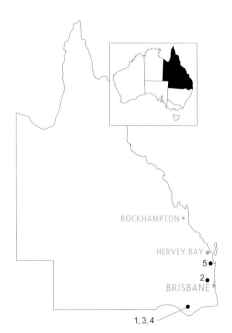

ROCKHAMPTON

HERVEY BAY

BRISBANE

1, 3, 4

QUEENSLAND

1. Just Red Wines PAGE 224
2370 Eukey Rd, Ballandean QLD 4382
Ph: (07) 4684 1322
www.justred.com.au

2. Mount England Estate PAGE 287
423 Wivenhoe-Somerset Rd,
* Fernvale QLD 4306*
Ph: (07) 5427 0042

3. Pyramids Road Wines PAGES 142, 143
25 Wyberba Lane,
* Wyberba via Ballandean QLD 4382*
Ph: (07) 4684 5151
www.pyramidsroad.com.au

4. Sirromet Wines PAGE 150
115 Anderson Rd, Ballandean QLD 4382
Ph: (07) 4684 1233
www.sirromet.com

5. The Little Morgue Winery PAGE 241
7 Rutherford Rd, Kulangoor QLD 4561
Ph: (07) 5441 5951
www.littlemorguewinery.com

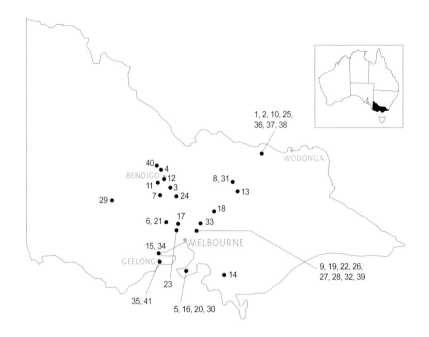

VICTORIA

**1. All Saints Estate and
  St Leonards Vineyard** PAGE 219
All Saints Rd, Wahgunyah VIC 3687
Ph: (02) 6035 2222
www.allsaintswine.com.au

2. Anderson Winery PAGE 220
Chiltern Rd, Rutherglen VIC 3685
Ph: (02) 6032 8111
www.andersonwinery.com.au

3. Armstead Estate PAGE 215
366 Moorabbee Rd, Knowsley VIC 3523
Ph: (03) 5439 1363
www.armsteadestate.com.au

4. Balgownie Estate PAGE 218
46 Hermitage Rd, Malden Gully VIC 3551
Ph: (03) 5449 6222
www.balgownieestate.com.au

5. B'darra Estate PAGE 289
1415 Stumpy Gully Rd, Moorooduc VIC 3933
Ph: (03) 5978 8447
www.bdarraestate.com.au

6. Big Shed Wines PAGE 100
1289 Malmsbury Rd, Glenlyon VIC 3461
Ph: (03) 5348 7825
www.bigshedwines.com.au

7. Bress Wine, Cider and Produce
  PAGES 34, 35
3894 Calder Hwy, Harcourt VIC 3453
Ph: (03) 5474 2262
www.bress.com.au

**8. Brown Brothers Milawa
  Vineyard** PAGE 133
*239 Milawa Bobinawarrah Rd,
  Milawa VIC 3678*
Ph: (03) 5720 5500
www.brownbrothers.com.au

9. Brumfield Winery PAGE 110
539 Queens Rd, Seville VIC 3139
Ph: (03) 5961 9081
www.brumfield.com.au

10. Bullers Winery Rutherglen PAGE 200
Three Chain Rd, Rutherglen VIC 3685
Ph: (03) 6032 9660
www.buller.com.au

11. Bullock Creek Vineyard PAGE 214
111 Belvoir Park Rd, Ravenswood North
* VIC 3453*
Ph: (03) 5435 3207
link via www.bendigowine.org.au

12. Château Dore' PAGE 203
303 Mandurang Rd, Mandurang VIC 3551
Ph: (03) 5439 5278

13. Chrismont Wines PAGES 108, 109
251 Upper King River Rd, Cheshunt VIC 3678
Ph: (03) 5729 8220
www.chrismont.com.au

14. Clair De Lune PAGE 48
8805 Sth Gippsland Hwy,
* Kardella South VIC 3951*
Ph: (03) 5655 1032
www.clairdelune.com.au

15. Clyde Park Vineyard & Bistro PAGE 11
2490 Midland Hwy, Bannockburn VIC 3331
Ph: (03) 5281 7274
www.clydepark.com.au

16. Crittenden Estate PAGE 242
25 Harrisons Rd, Dromana VIC 3936
Ph: (03) 5981 8322
www.crittendenwines.com.au

17. Curly Flat Vineyard PAGES 30–32
263 Collivers Rd, Lancefield VIC 3435
Ph: (03) 5429 1956
www.curlyflat.com

18. Delatite Winery PAGES 222, 223
Cnr Stoney's and Pollards Rds,
* Mansfield VIC 3722*
Ph: (03) 5775 2922
www.delatitewinery.com.au

19. Dominique Portet PAGE 154
870 Maroondah Hwy, Coldstream VIC 3770
Ph: (03) 5962 5760
www.dominiqueportet.com

20. Eldridge Estate PAGE 201
120 Arthurs Seat Rd, Red Hill VIC 3937
Ph: (03) 5989 2644
www.eldridge-estate.com.au

21. Ellender Estate PAGES 4, 58, BACK COVER
Leura Glen, 260 Green Gully Rd,
* Glenlyon VIC 3461*
Ph: (03) 5348 7785
www.ellenderwines.com.au

22. Fergusson Winery PAGE 229
84 Wills Rd, Yarra Glen VIC 3775
Ph: (03) 5965 2237
www.fergussonwinery.com.au

23. Hanging Rock Winery PAGE 212
88 Jim Rd, Newham VIC 3442
Ph: (03) 5427 0542
www.hangingrock.com.au

24. Idavue Estate PAGE 49
470 Northern Hwy, Heathcote VIC 3523
Ph: (03) 5433 3464
www.idavueestate.com

25. Jones Winery and Vineyard PAGE 28
61 Jones Rd, Rutherglen VIC 3685
Ph: (02) 6032 8496
www.joneswinery.com

26. Luke Lambert PAGE 55
PO Box 403, Yarra Glen VIC 3775
Ph: 0448 349 323
www.lukelambertwines.com.au

27. Medhurst Wines PAGE 159
24–26 Medhurst Rd, Gruyere VIC 3770
Ph: (03) 5964 9022
www.medhurstwines.com.au
www.redshedcafe.com.au

28. Morgan Vineyards PAGE 293
30 Davross Crt, Seville VIC 3139
Ph: (03) 5964 4807
www.morganvineyards.com.au

29. Mount Langi Ghiran PAGES 42, 43
80 Vine Rd, Ararat VIC 3377
Ph: (03) 5354 3207
www.langi.com.au

30. Principia PAGE 290
139 Main Creek Rd, Red Hill VIC 3937
Ph: (03) 5931 0010
www.principiawines.com.au

31. Sam Miranda King Valley
PAGES 156–158
1019 Snow Rd, King Valley VIC 3678
Ph: (03) 5727 3888
www.sammiranda.com.au

32. Seville Estate PAGES 44, 45
65 Linwood Rd, Seville VIC 3139
Ph: (03) 5964 2622
www.sevilleestate.com.au

33. Snobs Creek Estate PAGE 261
486 Goulburn Valley Hwy,
Snobs Creek VIC 3174
Ph: (03) 9596 3043
www.snobscreekvineyard.com.au

34. Spence PAGE 204
760 Burnside Rd, Murgheboluc VIC 3221
Ph: (03) 5265 1181
www.spencewines.com.au

35. St. Regis Vineyard PAGE 135
35 Princes Hwy, Waurn Ponds VIC 3216
Ph: (03) 5241 8406
www.stregis.com.au

36. Stanton & Killeen Wines PAGE 239
Jacks Rd, Rutherglen VIC 3685
Ph: (02) 6032 9457
www.stantonandkilleenwines.com.au

37. Valhalla Wines PAGE 165
163 All Saints Rd, Wahgunyah VIC 3687
Ph: (02) 6033 1438
www.valhallawines.com.au

38. Warrabilla Wines PAGE 134
6152 Murray Valley Hwy, Rutherglen
VIC 3685
Ph: (02) 6035 7242
www.warrabillawines.com.au

39. Warramate Wines PAGE 144
27 Maddens Lane, Gruyere VIC 3770
Ph: (03) 5964 9219
www.warramatewines.com.au

40. Water Wheel PAGES 46, 47
Lyndhurst St, Bridgewater on Loddon
VIC 3516
Ph: (03) 5437 3060
www.waterwheelwine.com

41. Waurn Ponds Estate PAGE 238
Deakin University, Pigdons Rd,
Waurn Ponds VIC 3216
Ph: (03) 5227 2143
www.waurnpondsestate.com.au

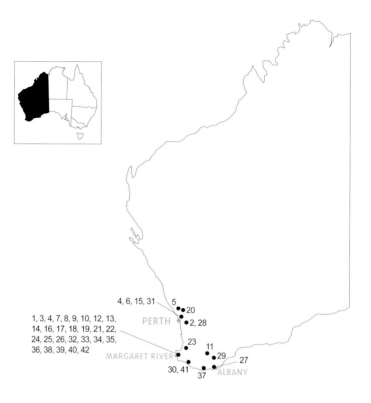

WESTERN AUSTRALIA

1. 3 Oceans Wine Co. PAGES 276–278
Bussell Hwy, Cowaramup WA 6284
Ph: (08) 9756 5656

2. Aldersyde Estate PAGE 280
226 Aldersyde Rd, Bickley WA 6076
Ph: (08) 9293 3309
www.aldersyde.com.au

3. Beckett's Flat PAGE 243
49 Beckett Rd, Metricup WA 6280
Ph: (08) 9755 7402
www.beckettsflat.com.au

4. Bella Ridge Estate PAGE 141
78 Campersic Rd, Herne Hill WA 6056
Ph: (08) 9250 4962
www.bellaridge.com.au

5. Berrigan Wines PAGE 191
136 Creighton Rd, Gingin WA 6503
Ph: (08) 9383 7526
www.berriganwines.com.au

**6. Black Swan Winery
  and Restaurant** PAGES 250, 251
8600 West Swan Rd, Henley Brook WA 6055
Ph: (08) 9296 6090
www.blackswanwines.com.au

7. Cape Naturaliste Vineyard PAGES 1, 54
1 Coley Rd, Yallingup WA 6282
Ph: (08) 9755 2538
www.capenaturalistevineyard.com.au

8. Clairault Wines PAGE 111
3277 Caves Rd, Wilyabrup WA 6281
Ph: (08) 9755 6655
www.clairaultwines.com.au

9. Coward & Black at Providore PAGE 36
448 Harmans South Rd, Wilyabrup WA 6280
Ph: (08) 9755 6355
www.cowardandblack.com.au

10. Fermoy Estate PAGES 96, 97
Metricup Rd, Wilyabrup WA 6280
Ph: (08) 9755 6285
www.fermoy.com.au

11. Ferngrove Estate PAGE 288
276 Ferngrove Rd, Frankland WA 6396
Ph: (08) 9855 2378
www.ferngrove.com.au

12. Flametree Wines PAGES 126, 127
Cnr Caves Rd and Chain Ave,
   Dunsborough WA 6281
Ph: (08) 9756 8577
www.flametreewines.com

13. Flying Fish Cove PAGE 286
Caves Rd, Wilyabrup WA 6281
Ph: (08) 9755 6600
www.flyingfishcove.com

14. Happs and Three Hills PAGE 284
575 Commonage Rd, Dunsborough WA 6281
Ph: (08) 9755 3300
www.happs.com.au

15. Harris Organic Wines PAGE 114
179 Memorial Ave, Baskerville WA 6056
Ph: (08) 9296 0216
www.harrisorganicwine.com

16. Hay Shed Hill PAGE 132
511 Harmans Mill Rd, Wilyabrup WA 6284
Ph: (08) 9755 6046
www.hayshedhill.com.au

17. Island Brook Estate PAGE 160
7388 Bussell Hwy, Metricup WA 6280
Ph: (08) 9755 7501
www.islandbrook.com.au

18. Juniper Estate PAGE 14
Harman's Rd South, Cowaramup WA 6284
Ph: (08) 9755 9000
www.juniperestate.com.au

19. Knee Deep Wines PAGE 184
Lot 61, Johnson Rd, Margaret River WA 6280
Ph: (08) 9755 6776
www.kneedeepwines.com.au

20. Kyotmunga Estate PAGE 13
287 Chittering Valley Rd,
   Lower Chittering WA 6084
Ph: (08) 9571 8001
www.kyotmunga.com.au

21. Laurance Wines PAGE 183
3518 Caves Rd, Wilyabrup WA 6282
Ph: (08) 9755 6199
www.laurancewines.com

22. Leeuwin Estate PAGES 98, 99
Stevens Rd, Margaret River WA 6285
Ph: (08) 9759 0000
www.leeuwinestate.com.au

23. Mandalay Road PAGE 272
254 Mandalay Rd, Glen Mervyn WA 6239
Ph: (08) 9732 2006
www.mandalayroad.com.au

24. Margaret River Vineyard Estate
   PAGE 273
Clews Rd, Cowaramup WA 6284
Ph: (08) 9755 5054

25. Marri Wood Park PAGE 207
Cnr Caves and Whittle Rds,
   Yallingup WA 6282
Ph: (08) 9755 2343

26. Merops PAGE 181
5992 Caves Rd, Margaret River WA 6285
Ph: (08) 9757 9195
www.meropswines.com.au

27. Oranje Tractor PAGE 33
198 Link Rd, Albany WA 6330
Ph: (08) 9842 5175
www.oranjetractor.com

28. Piesse Brook Winery PAGE 281
226 Aldersyde Rd, Bickley WA 6076
Ph: (08) 9293 3309

29. Plantagenet Wines PAGES 208, 209
Lot 45, Albany Hwy, Mount Barker WA 6324
Ph: (08) 9851 3111
www.plantagenetwines.com

30. Silkwood Wines PAGE 292
5204 Channybearup Rd,
   Pemberton WA 6260
Ph: (08) 9776 1584
www.silkwoodwines.com.au

31. Sittella Winery PAGE 176
100 Barrett St, Herne Hill WA 6056
Ph: (08) 9296 2600
www.sittella.com.au

32. Stella Bella PAGE 296
Lot 16, Rosabrook Rd,
  Margaret River WA 6285
Ph: (08) 9757 6377
www.stellabella.com.au

33. Swings & Roundabouts PAGE 256
Caves Rd, Yallingup WA 6282
Ph: (08) 9756 6735
www.swings.com.au

34. Tassell Park Wines PAGE 291
Treeton Rd, Cowaramup WA 6284
Ph: (08) 9755 5440
www.tassellparkwines.com

35. Voyager Estate PAGES 61–83
Stevens Rd, Margaret River WA 6285
Ph: (08) 9757 6354
www.voyagerestate.com.au

36. Watershed Premium Wines PAGE 20
Cnr Bussell Hwy and Darch Rd,
  Margaret River WA 6285
Ph: (08) 9758 8633
www.watershedwines.com.au

37. Whitfield Estate PAGES 104, 105
198 McIntyre Rd, Denmark WA 6333
Ph: (08) 9840 9016
www.whitfieldestate.com.au

38. Willespie PAGES 24–26
555 Harmans Mill Rd, Wilyabrup WA 6280
Ph: (08) 9755 6248
www.willespie.com.au

39. Wills Domain PAGE 285
Cnr Brash and Abbey Farm Rds,
  Yallingup WA 6282
Ph: (08) 9755 2327
www.willsdomain.com.au

40. Windows Margaret River
  PAGES 178, 179
4 Quininup Rd, Yallingup WA 6282
Ph: (08) 9755 2719
www.windowsmargaretriver.com

41. Wine & Truffle Co. PAGE 177
Seven Day Rd, Manjimup WA 6258
Ph: (08) 9777 2474
www.wineandtruffle.com.au

42. Woody Nook PAGES 252, 253
506 Metricup Rd, Wilyabrup WA 6280
Ph: (08) 9755 7547
www.woodynook.com.au

WINE DOGS BREED INDEX

THANK YOU...

Wine Dogs would like to thank the following people who helped us on our journey.

Thanks to Peter 'Rock Giant' Herring, Huon Hooke, Norm, Pat, Jim and Isobel for all their support (and great dog-sitting skills), Jennifer Grieve from Wine Dogs Italy, Richard Hogan from ZooWines, Jim Kelly, Vicki Wild and Martin Benn from Sepia Restaurant & Wine Bar, Robert, Vanessa, Josh and the gang from Australia's premier Italian restaurant – Il Piave. We also have a fabulous network of friends (too many to mention), whose constant support and help have made this book a lot easier to produce.

To our wonderful huskies, Tarka and Stella, for bringing a smile to our faces when we needed it most.

Along our travels we were helped and encouraged by many wonderful people including Liz Russell and Andrew Guard from Torbreck Vintners, Peter and Margaret Lehmann, Dave Lehmann, Penny McGann from Voyager Estate, Matt Burton from Wandin Valley Estate, Damien Harris from Totino Estate, Sean Blocksidge from The Margaret River Discovery Company, Eliza Brown from All Saints Estate, Denis Mifsud from Wino's Margaret River, Patrick Coward from Coward & Black at Providore, Jim Ross at Merops, Mark and Mandy Creed, Merry Canavan and Roger Duance from Hummocks Station, Mike Christophersen from Seppeltsfield Wines, Colin Hopkins at Sunset Winery Kangaroo Island, Terry Jongebloed from Clyde Park for the sensational wood-fire pizza, Louise Fergusson at Fergusson Winery for the superb breakfast, Margaret and Graham Van Der Meulen for a great lunch that was difficult to move on from...

When staying in the Barossa, Wine Dogs chooses to stay at the fantastic Belle Escapes cottages, located conveniently in the heart of the Barossa and only staggering distance from all your favourite cellar doors.

When in the Hunter Valley, Wine Dogs chooses to stay at Wandin Valley Estate in the greener pastures of Lovedale in the Lower Hunter Valley. The beautiful self-contained villas are set amongst the vines and are conveniently located at the gateway of the Hunter wine country – enjoy the great wine as you explore this unique estate.

For a unique stay in a historical sheep station we stayed at Hummocks Station in Snowtown that is a stone's throw from Clare Valley. It's full of rustic, authentic character and where the stars at night fill the sky as big as any Texan night.

We would like to express our gratitude to all the wineries that gifted us with some of the most amazing wines you could ever taste, including Home Hill Winery, Josef Chromy, Puddleduck, Meadowbank, Beckett's Flat, Bella Ridge Estate, Black Swan Winery, Coward & Black at Providore, Fermoy Estate, Hay Shed Hill, Kyotmunga Estate, Mandalay Road, Marri Wood Park, Oranje Tractor, Plantagenet Wines, Sittella Winery, Voyager Estate, Watershed Premium Wines, Whitfield Estate, Windows Margaret River, Woody Nook, Burk Salter Wines, Crabtree Wines, Creed of Barossa, Gibsons Barossa Vale, Kay Brothers, Noon Winery, Patrick T Wines, Smallfry Wines, Sunset Winery Kangaroo Island, The Poplars, Torbreck Vintners, Totino Estate, Vincognita Wines, Zema Estate, Armstead Estate, B'Darra Estate, Bress Wine, Bullers Winery Rutherglen, Bullock Creek Vineyard, Curly Flat Vineyard, Dominique Portet, Ellender Estate, Idavue Estate, Luke Lambert Wines, Mount Langi Ghiran, Principia, Seville Estate, Snobs Creek Estate, Spence, St. Regis Vineyard, Warrabilla, Water Wheel, Just Red Wines, Mount England Estate, Burrundulla Vineyards, Catherine Vale, Cumulus Wines: Rolling and Climbing, Gundagai Wines, Kevin Sobels Wines, Krinklewood, Mabrook Estate, Philip Shaw Wines, Wandin Valley Estate and Wirral Grange Vineyard.

And we must draw special attention to the wonderful generosity and hospitality offered to us by Voyager Estate in the Margaret River. We really appreciate all their support of Wine Dogs. This iconic winery is truly one of the great wine estates of the world.

Special thanks to all our contributors: Nick Ryan, Nick Stock, Greg Duncan Powell, Zar Brooks, Peter Forrestal, Zoe Williams, Tory Shepherd, Warren Hately, Matthew Jukes, Peter and Margaret Lehmann, Jason Hoy and Dave Powell for their excellently crafted stories and support. Thanks guys.

To Catherine 'Demon' Rendell for her amazing Wine Dogs website work, Melinda McFadden, Lily Li and Vicky Fisher for helping make Wine Dogs great.

Our apologies to the wineries that we didn't visit. Please contact us for entry into the next edition.

WINE DOGS AUSTRALIA 3: If your winery and woofer missed out on appearing in this edition please contact us at entries@winedogs.com and register for the Wine Dogs Australia 3. We'll look forward to hearing from you. Woof!